MW01592401

HOW TO CHANGE YOUR MIND

How to Switch On Your Mind to Change
Habits, Stop Worrying, Relieve Anxiety and
Regain Control of Your Life

DAN COLLINS

Summary

Chapter 1: Why Human Mind requires Help

The mind is the arrangement of intellectual faculties, including consciousness, creative mind, perception, reasoning, judgment, speech, and memory, which are located in the cerebrum (including the focal sensory system in some cases). It is defined generally as the workforce of the contemplations and consciousness of an individual. This retains the strength of creative mind, appreciation, and gratitude, and is responsible for planning thoughts, plans, and events.

The mind is also represented as the continuous flow where experiences of the senses and cognitive wonders often display signs of change.

Mental states can be completely aware or unaware. We can respond to circumstances with excitement without controlling why we respond. The mental state has a similar physiology, experienced in the physical body as a positive or negative effect. For example, the mental state of anxiety makes you create hormones of stress.

A healthy mind will help you find your way through life, from birth through puberty, through years of high school, adulthood, and into an older age. Mind is the earth's greatest supernatural event. The mind is the safety of mind. It will be simpler and more focused, the musings will be stronger. But it should be planned and kept balanced with the end goal for the mind to think and work properly.

Mental health requires happiness in the mind, heart, and in the social. It means that it influences how every day we act, think, and carry on. The mental health also leads to the basic cycle of leadership, how we respond to stress, and how we connect in our lives with others.

There are steps that you can take to continuously strengthen your mental health. Simple things like working out, having a fair and safe meal, opening up to other people in your life, taking a break when you need to, remembering what you enjoy, and getting a decent night's rest will help boost your passionate wellbeing.

1.1   What are the problems of mental health?

Mental health is like physical health in many ways: everyone has it, and we need to look after it.

Good mental health is generally capable of thinking, feeling, and reacting in the ways you need and want to live your life. Yet if you go through a time of poor mental health, you can find it difficult, or even impossible, to cope with the ways you sometimes think, feel, or respond. This can feel just as bad as a physical illness, or even worse.

In any given year, mental health problems affect about one in four people. They range from everyday problems, such as depression and anxiety, to rarer problems such as schizophrenia and bipolar disorder.

1.2 Am I the only one that feels like this how to overcome this?

Experiencing a question of mental health is often disturbing, frustrating, and terrifying particularly at first. If you get unwell, you may think it's a sign of weakness, or you're "losing your mind."

Such beliefs are often compounded by the stereotypical (and often unrealistic) manner in which people with mental health issues are shown on television, in films, and the media. This may stop you from talking or seeking help with your problems. This, in turn, is likely to make you feel more distressed and isolated.

Mental health problems, however, are a collective human experience in reality.

Many people know someone who has had a problem with mental health. They can happen from all walks of life to all kinds of people. And you may get better when you find a mix of self-care, medication, so help that works for you.

Here are some other mental disorders

Anger

Sometimes we all feel angry–it's part of being a human being. Anger is a natural, healthy emotion that we may experience when we think: insulted, upset disabled, or unfairly treated. It is not inherently an' evil' emotion; in reality, it can be useful often. For example: feeling angry about anything can help us identify problems or things that are hurting us motivate us to create change.

1.3   When anger is a problem, how to solve them?

Anger becomes a problem only if it gets out of control and hurts you or the people around you. This can occur when:

- You express your rage frequently by unhelpful or destructive behavior
- your passion harms your overall mental and physical
- Violence becomes your go-to emotion, suppresses your ability to feel other emotions that you have not learned sound ways to express your anger

What is unhelpful angry behavior?

Not everyone is in the same manner expressing anger. For example, some unhelpful ways you may have learned to express anger include outward aggression and violence such as shouting, swearing, slamming doors, hitting or throwing things, and being physically violent or verbally abusive and threatening others.

Inward violence-such as convincing yourself that you hate yourself, refusing your basic needs (such as food or things that could make you happy), closing yourself off from the world, and hurting yourself.

Non-violent or passive aggression: ignoring people or refusing to talk to them, refusing to do tasks, or doing things deliberately poorly, late or at the last possible minute, and being sarcastic or sulky without saying anything explicitly aggressive or angry.

Bipolar disorder

Bipolar disorder is a problem of mental health that affects your mood primarily. If you have bipolar disorder, you more are likely to experience times: manic or hypomanic episodes (feeling high) depressive episodes (feeling low) during manic or depressed periods, probably some psychotic symptoms.

Everyone has different moods, but these shifts can be very distressing in bipolar disorder and have a significant impact on your life. You can think that your feelings are pressing, high and low and that your mood swings are disturbing.

Loneliness

From time to time, we all feel lonely. Loneliness feelings are private, so it will be unique for everyone to experience loneliness.

The feelings we get when our need for satisfying social contact and relationships is not fulfilled is a standard description of loneliness. Yet isolation is not the same as being alone at all times.

You may have to choose to be alone and live happily without having a lot of contact with others, while others may find this a lonely experience.

Or you may have a lot of social interaction, or you may be in a relationship or part of a family, and still feel lonely–particularly if you don't think that the people around you understand or care about you (see our details on the causes of loneliness).

Is loneliness a question for mental health?

Feeling lonely is not just a mental health problem in itself, but there is a clear connection between the two. Having a problem with mental health can increase your chances of feeling lonely.

Or you may experience social phobia–also known as social anxiety–and find it challenging to engage in day-to-day activities involving other people, leading to a lack of meaningful social contact and loneliness feelings.

1.4   What causes loneliness?

Loneliness has many different causes; those vary from person to person. We don't always understand what an experience is about, which makes us feel lonely.

For some people, specific life events may mean they feel lonely, such as: experiencing a bereavement going through a relationship break-up retiring and losing the social contact you had at work changing jobs and feeling isolated from your co-workers starting at university moving to a new area or country without family, friends or community networks.

Some people find that at certain times of the year, like around Christmas, they feel lonely.

Some research suggests that individuals who live or belong to specific groups under certain conditions are more likely to be vulnerable to loneliness. For example, if you have no friends or family who are alienated from your family, you are a single parent or care for someone else–you may find it difficult to maintain a social life belonging to minority groups and living in an area without others of similar background who are excluded from social activities due to mobility problems or lack of money due to discrimination and stigma.

Other mental disorders:

Suicidal feelings:

Suicide is the way of taking your own life deliberately. Suicidal feelings can range from stressing about abstract thinking about ending your life to believing like people would be better off without you, thinking about suicide methods, or making clear plans to take your own life. When you feel suicidal, these feelings can scare you or confuse you. You're not alone, though. At some point in their lifetime, most people think of suicide.

1.5 How to control the wrong feeling?

The feelings experienced by everyone are unique to them. You may feel unable to cope with the complicated and persistent feelings that you encounter. You may feel less like you're going to die and more like you can't live your life.

Such emotions may or may fluctuate over time from moment to moment. And it's normal not to understand why this is how you feel.

Here are some thoughts, feelings, and experiences that you may experience when you feel unhappy:

- How you might think or feel what you might experience
- Hopeless, like there's no point in living
- Tearful and overwhelmed by negative thoughts
- Unbearable pain that you can't imagine ending
- Useless, unwanted or unnecessary by others
- Desperate, as if it were desperate.

Seasonal affective disorder (SAD)

Seasonal affective disorder (SAD) is a kind of depression you feel during seasons or seasons. Depression is a long-lasting low mood that affects your daily life.

If you have SAD, particularly during some seasons, or due to certain types of weather, you will experience depression.

It's like making your black cloud mobile.

Changing seasons and weather, and having periods of the year when you feel more or less relaxed, is normal to be affected. For example, you may find that when it gets colder or warmer, your mood or energy levels drop, or you may notice changes in your patterns of sleeping or eating.

But if your emotions interfere with your daily life, it may be a sign that you have depression–and if they keep coming back at the same time of year, doctors might call it seasonal affective disorder or' seasonal depression.'

What are SAD's symptoms?

You can experience some of the signs and symptoms below if you have SAD. But it's different for different people, and can vary season to season, so you might also have other kinds of feelings which aren't listed here: lack of energy

Finding it hard to concentrate Not wanting to see people

- Sleep problems, such as sleeping more or less than usual,
- Difficulty waking up, or trouble falling or staying asleep
- Feeling sad, low, tearful, guilty or hopeless
- Changes in your appetite, for example, handling more hungry or wanting more snacks being more prone to physical health problems, such as colds, infections or other illnesses
- Losing interest in sex or physical contact
- Suicidal feelings
- Other symptoms of depression

Chapter 2: Anxiety

2.1   What is anxiety and how to overcome this situation?

Anxiety is an emotion that is natural and often good. If a person feels excessive levels of anxiety regularly, however, it may become a medical disorder.

Anxiety disorders form a class of conditions of mental health that lead to excessive nervousness, anxiety, anticipation, and worry. Such diseases change how a person experiences emotions and behaviors, and also cause physical symptoms. Mild anxiety can be ambiguous and disturbing, while severe anxiety can have a severe impact on daily living.

In the US, anxiety disorders affect 40 million people. It is the country's most popular group of mental illness. Nevertheless, care is given to only 36.9 percent of people with an anxiety disorder.

Anxiety is described by the American Psychological Association (APA) as "an emotion characterized by feelings of distress, worried thoughts, and physical changes such as increased blood pressure." Knowing the difference between normal anxiety feelings and an anxiety disorder requiring medical treatment may help a person recognize and manage the condition.

2.2   When do you need treatment for anxiety?

It is not always a medical condition, but depression can cause distress. Anxiety feelings are not only natural but necessary for survival when a person faces potentially harmful or troubling causes.

The approach of predators and incoming danger has been setting off alarms in the body since the earliest days of humanity, allowing for evasive action. These are the alerts.

Anxiety Feelings of anxiety are not only natural but necessary for survival when a person faces potentially harmful or troubling causes.

The presence of predators and emerging threat has been setting alarms in the body since humanity's earliest days and allowing for evasive action. Such warnings are apparent in the form of increased breathing, sweating, and ambient sensitivity.

The risk induces an adrenaline rush, a hormone and chemical signal in the brain, which in effect activates such nervous responses in a process called the "fight-or-flight" response. It prepares humans to tackle or avoid any potential safety hazards physically. For many people, fleeing from larger animals and imminent danger is less of a concern than it would have been for early humans.

Anxiety disorders sometimes, the length and severity of anxiety may be out of proportion with the original cause or stressor. Physical symptoms may also occur, such as increased blood pressure and vomiting. Such reactions shift into an anxiety disorder beyond depression.

The APA describes a person with anxiety disorder as having "recurring intrusive thoughts or fears." It may interfere with everyday function when anxiety reaches the level of a disease.

Symptoms While a number of different conditions are anxiety disorders, the symptoms of widespread anxiety disorder (GAD) will often include the following: restlessness, and feeling "on-edge" uncontrollable feelings of concern, increased irritability concentration difficulties sleeping difficulties, such as issues falling and staying asleep While these symptoms may be familiar to e GAD may be a vague, disturbing fear or a more severe anxiety that disrupts everyday life.

Types

The Mental Health Conditions Diagnostic and Statistical Manual: Fifth

Edition (DSM-V) classifies several significant categories of anxiety disorders.

Anxiety disorders included obsessive-compulsive disorder (OCD) and post- traumatic stress disorder (PTSD) in previous editions of DSM, as well as acute stress disorder. The guide, however, is no longer grouping Trusted Source under depression, such as mental health problems.

The following diagnoses now include anxiety disorders.

Generalized anxiety disorder:

This is a persistent condition that causes severe, long-lasting anxiety and fears regarding non-specific events, things, and circumstances in life. GAD is the most common anxiety disorder, and the cause of their anxiety is not always known by people with the disease.

Panic Disorder:

The panic condition is characterized by brief and unexpected attacks of extreme fear and anxiety. Such attacks can result in trembling, confusion, dizziness, vomiting, and difficulty breathing. Panic attacks tend to take place and intensify quickly, peaking 10 minutes later. A panic attack could last for hours, though.

Symptoms:

Panic symptoms usually occur after traumatic events or excessive stress, but without a cause can also occur. A person who has a panic attack may view it as a life-threatening illness and may make drastic behavioral changes to avoid future attacks.

Personal phobia:

This is an irrational fear or avoidance of an event or circumstance in general. Phobias are not like other anxiety disorders because they are linked to a particular cause.

A person with a phobia may identify fear as illogical or severe but may remain unable to manage anxiety about the cause. Triggers for a phobia range from everyday objects to situations and animals.

Agoraphobia:

This is a fear and avoidance of locations, things, or circumstances from which to flee or in which help would not be available if a person was stuck. People sometimes misinterpret this disorder as a phobia of outdoor and open spaces, but it's not that easy. An agoraphobic person may be afraid to leave home or use elevators or public transportation.

Selective Mutism:

This is a type of anxiety encountered by some adolescents, where they are unable to communicate in specific locations or situations, such as university, although they may have outstanding verbal communication skills with familiar individuals. It is a form of social phobia that is severe.

2.3   How to stay positive and make your mind free from stress and anxiety

1.   Consider the optimistic point of view in a negative situation:

In my experience, one of the easiest but most successful ways of building a more positive outlook has been to pose as often as possible, more constructive questions.

If I'm in what seems like a negative situation, maybe I've been careless, made a mistake, lost or fallen in some way, then I like to ask myself questions such as: What's one thing about this situation that's optimistic or good?

What is a chance in this situation?

Doing so is much better than I used to do in situations like this. Because I usually wondered back then how much I sucked and how things could get worse now.

However, I don't always immediately use these questions.

Perhaps I need a little time before I can do that to process the thoughts and feelings that emerge in the situation.

When you're still in an emotional turmoil or a little surprised trying to force positive thinking usually doesn't work that well.

2.   Cultivate and live in a positive environment:

What you choose to spend your time with and the feedback you get from far away will have a significant impact on your outlook.

It is essential to have influences in your life that support you and lift you rather than drag you down to remain positive.

So consider carefully what you're going to let in your mind.

For example, you can ask yourself:

Who are the three most negative people with whom I spend time? What are the 3 most negative information sources I spend time on?

Find the answers. Then think about how this week you can start to spend less time with one of those individuals or sources of information.

3.   Go slowly:

I find that things don't go too well when I go too fast when I try to think, chat, eat, and walk around in my world quickly.

Stress is on the rise. Negative thoughts about just about anything are starting to get well, and I feel like my power is weakening.

But if I slow down for just a few minutes, even if by driving, talking, and eating slowly, I have to force it, then my mind and body always calms down. The optimistic and constructive perspective becomes more comfortable and more natural to think things through.

4.   Don't make a mountain out of a molehill:

Losing focus is very easy, particularly if you're stressed, and you're moving too quickly.

A quick three-step approach to deal with these situations so that they don't get out of control is: Say stop: yell "STOP! "And" NOPE, we don't go down that road again! "As soon as this kind of thought starts to spin in your mind.

Breathe:

Sit down and be still after you've disrupted your thoughts by shouting. To calm your mind and body down, relax with your stomach, and concentrate on just your in-breaths and out-breaths for a minute or two.

Refocus:

Ask your mountain-building thoughts by speaking to someone close to you and having a more rounded view of the situation by actually winding up or getting your feedback. Or ask yourself this to broaden your perspective and chill out:

Is this going to happen in five years? Or even for five weeks?

5.   Do not allow abstract doubts to stop you from doing what you want:

You may want to take a chance in life at times. Start a new habit that feels foreign, side by side with your own company, or ask for a date.

If you want to do one of these things, a common trap is to get stuck in abstract worries and what might happen when you take action.

And so the mind is spinning wildly fueled by terror, generating visions of nightmare and plenty of self-doubt.

I know I was there a lot of times.

And I learned to ask myself this: frankly, what could be the worst?

I always spend a bit of time trying to figure out what I could do if that ever happens to be pretty unlikely.

Over the years, I have found that the worst thing that could happen is typically not as terrifying as the nightmare that my fear-fueled imagination would make.

It doesn't take a lot of time or effort to find clarification in this way, and it can help you avoid a lot of mind-made pain. And help you get out of your comfort zone and take the opportunity.

6. Bring meaning and positivity to the life of someone else:

You expect to get back from the world and the people in it what you put out. Not all of them. And not at all times.

But it matters a lot what you send out.

What you are giving them and how you are treating them is what you are going to get back. And they're treating others and also tend to have a significant effect on how you treat and think about yourself.

For example, give value and spread the positivity: uh, help out: give a hand as you pass. Give your car a ride to a friend. If he or she needs details, search it on Google or ask a friend of yours to help. Or start a blog or podcast and share your life's support.

Listening alone: people often don't want any direct help, They want somebody to be there and look as they're selling for a while.

Mood-boosting: smile. Give hugs if necessary. If you're hanging out with a friend, play uplifting music or recommend an inspirational film for your movie night. Or inspire others to go through a tough time when they've had a bad day.

7. Daily exercise and eat and sleep well:

This is, of course, very clear.

But I know the signs, significant impact of a good night's sleep or good workout when my thoughts are pessimistic, and inside I have a lot of tensions.

And I know how much easier it is when my stomach is not full to think clearly and optimistically.

And I strongly recommend that you be careful about these simple habits that may sound repetitive. Because either way, they have an enormous effect, depending on how you handle them.

8. Learn to criticize healthily:

Fear of criticism is one of the most common concerns. It can keep people from doing what they want in life.

Because it can damage someone's mouth or email with anger, and it's about you. And being dismissed can sting a bit.

But if you want to move on what you want to do deep down, then criticism is almost inevitable. The key, therefore, is to learn how to handle it healthier.

By doing so, your fear will diminish, and if you get criticized, it will hurt less.

When I get some feedback, I usually use four measures. Maybe they can also help you out:

Step 1: Don't answer right away: when you're angry, upset, or upset, it's time to calm down a little before you answer. Take at least a few deep breaths or some time before you respond to the message.

Step 2: Listen to the criticism: try to stay open and level-headed and find out how this message can help you.

Ask yourself: Can I benefit from this critique one thing? Is there something I might not like to learn here but could support me?

Step 3: Remember, it's not always about you to criticize: some criticism is helpful. Some are just threats or someone who lashes out because they have a bad day, a bad year, or a job.

I try to be understanding to lessen the sting of such criticism—often furious and overly critical in an unconstructive way. I think this person may not feel so good at the moment.

Step 4: Answer or let go: I try to keep my answer level-headed and kind regardless of the content of a letter, for example. I may add one or two questions to get more useful specific feedback.

And if they don't answer or I just got a nasty attack, it's time to remove it and let go of that situation.

9.   If something gets under your skin, then know what to do:

Something can still get under your skin and damage you sometimes even if you are using the above measure.

Two aspects that helped me with this struggle are: Let it out: getting this problem out into the light speaking to someone familiar can be very helpful

in seeing it for what it is and finding a healthier view of the situation. Improve your self-esteem: Over the years, I have found that things drag me down less with a stronger self-esteem and no longer ruin my day. Negativity from others bounces me a lot more often than not.

10.   Start your day positively:

Generally, set the tone for the rest of your day when you start your day. So be careful how you're spending your days.

If you go at full speed, lose your mind in future troubles, then the stress, perceived power loss over your life and negative thoughts will ramp up rapidly.

When, on the other hand, you start your day by moving slowly, having an uplifting talk with your family or friend, or you spend some time reading or listening to motivational and supportive things or podcasts during your breakfast or bus ride to work, that can make a big difference to how the whole day goes.

11.   Once you spend your time

In the present moment, it becomes so much easier to access positive emotions and stay realistic about what you can do about something in your life.

You've spent a lot of time doing things when you're stuck in the past or the future, like so many of us, so worries get bigger quickly. So past failures drag you down into pessimism, so errors that are endlessly replayed in your mind. When you get stuck in the past or the future, like so many of us, you've spent a lot of time doing things, so worries get bigger quickly. And past failures and errors that are endlessly replayed in your mind drag you down into pessimism.

By moving slowly through your morning and hopefully through much of the rest of your day, staying attentively becomes more comfortable at the moment you're feeling

Another simple way to reconnect with the moment you're in and once again concentrate your full attention on what's going on around you right now with all your senses for a minute or two. See that. See that. Yeah, listen to it. Smell. Smell. Feel the sun on your body, the rain, or the cold wind.

It may sound like something small and insignificant to do. But for the rest of your day, this simplifying reconnection with the moment can have a very positive effect.

Disorder of social anxiety or social phobia

This is a fear of other people's negative opinion in social situations and public embarrassment. Social anxiety disorder includes a variety of emotions, including scenario fear, fear of intimacy, and anxiety about shame or rejection.

Such a condition can result in people avoiding social interactions and human contact to the point that everyday life is complicated.

Separation anxiety disorder

High levels of anxiety describe separation anxiety disorder after separation from a person or place that offers feelings of comfort or protection. Divorce can sometimes lead to symptoms of anxiety.

Origins Complicated are the origins of anxiety disorders. Many may happen at once, some may lead to others, and some may not lead to a condition of anxiety unless there is one.

Causes:

Possible causes include environmental stressors, such as work problems, relationship problems, or family genetics, as individuals with family members with an anxiety disorder are more likely to experience medical factors on their own, such as the symptoms of another disease, the effects of medication, or the stress of intensive surgery or prolonged brain chemistry recovery.

2.4   Treatment

A mixture of psychotherapy, behavioral therapy, or medicine may consist of therapies.

Dependence on alcohol, depression, or other disorders can sometimes have such a strong effect on psychological well-being that the treatment of an anxiety disorder must wait until any underlying conditions are managed.

Yoga self-treatment can reduce an anxiety disorder's effects.

Treatment At Home

In some cases, without medical supervision, a person may treat an anxiety disorder at home. Nonetheless, for severe or long-term anxiety disorders, this may not be successful.

There are several strategies and activities to help a person deal with anxiety disorders that are milder, more concentrated, or shorter-term, including stress management: learning to manage stress may help limit potential triggers. Organize any pressures and deadlines that may arise, compile lists to make daunting tasks more manageable, and commit to taking time off study or work.

Relaxation Techniques:

Simple activities can help relieve anxiety's mental and physical signs. These techniques include meditation, exercises for deep breathing, long baths, dark resting, and yoga.

Exercises to substitute negative thoughts with positive ones:

List the negative thoughts that may be circulating as a result of anxiety, and write a list next to it that includes positive, plausible thoughts to replace them. Having a mental image of facing a particular fear effectively and overcoming it can also be helpful if the symptoms of anxiety related to a specific cause, such as a phobia.

Support Network:

Contact ordinary supporting people, such as a family member or friend. Local and online support group resources may also be available.

Exercise:

Physical exercise can improve the self-image and release into the brain chemicals that trigger positive feelings.

Therapy Clinical therapy is a common way to treat depression. This may include cognitive-behavioral therapy (CBT), psychotherapy, or a therapy combination.

CBT

This method of psychotherapy aims at identifying and modifying negative patterns of thought that form the basis of nervous and upsetting feelings. In the meantime, CBT therapists aim to reduce distorted thinking and change the way people respond to anxiety-causing stimuli or circumstances. A psychotherapist treating panic disorder with CBT, for instance, should try to reinforce the idea that panic attacks are not really heart attacks. CBT may be part of sensitivity to fears and causes. It allows people to overcome their fears and helps to reduce their exposure to their usual anxiety causes.

Medications

A person can support multiple types of medication to manage anxiety. Antidepressants, benzodiazepines, tricyclic's, and beta-blockers are medications that may control some of the physical and mental symptoms.

Benzodiazepines:

Many people with depression may be prescribed by a doctor, but they may be highly addictive. Except for somnolence and potential addiction, these medications appear to have few side effects. Diazepam, or Valium, is an example of benzodiazepine commonly prescribed.

Antidepressants:

They usually help with anxiety, although they are often directed at depression. People frequently use serotonin reuptake inhibitors (SSRIs), which have fewer side effects than older antidepressants but are likely to cause jitters, vomiting, and sexual dysfunction once therapy begins. Fluoxetine, or Prozac, and citalopram, or Celexa, are other antidepressants.

Tricyclic's:

This is a class of older medications than SSRIs that provide advantages for most other than OCD anxiety disorders. Such medicines can cause side effects such as dizziness, somnolence, dry mouth, and weight gain. Two examples of tricyclics are imipramine and clomipramine.

2.5   Other medicines that a person may use to treat anxiety include

Beta-blockers buspirone monoamine oxidase inhibitors (MAOIs) Seek medical advice if the adverse effects of any prescription medicines are serious.

Prevention

There are ways to reduce the risk of symptoms of anxiety. Remember that depression is a standard variable in everyday life, and feeling it does not always suggest a mental health disorder.

To help moderate nervous feelings, take the following steps:

- Increasing the consumption of caffeine, coffee, cola, and chocolate.
- Test with a doctor or pharmacist for any substances that may make anxiety symptoms worse before using over-the-counter (OTC) or herbal remedies.
- Keep a healthy diet.
- Maintain a regular pattern of sleep.
- Avoid alcohol, marijuana, and other substances for pleasure.

Takeaway Anxiety is not a medical condition itself, but a normal emotion that is vital to survival when a person faces risk.

When this response is excessive or out of proportion to the stimulus that triggers it, an anxiety disorder occurs. There are several forms of anxiety disorder, including fear, phobia, and social anxiety disorder.

Treatment involves, along with self-help steps, a combination of different types of therapy, medicine, and counseling

Chapter 3: Depression

3.1 What is depression and how to handle this?

Sadness, feeling down, losing interest, and having fun in everyday activities- these are signs that we are all familiar with. But if they continue and seriously affect our lives, it can be depression.

7.6 percent of people over the age of 12 have depression in any 2 weeks, according to the Centers for Disease Control and Prevention (CDC). This is remarkable and demonstrates the scale of the problem.

Depression is the world's most common disease and the leading cause of disability, according to the World Health Organization (WHO). They say that depression affects 350 million people worldwide.

Quick depression facts:

- Depression tends to be more prevalent in women than men.
- Signs include lack of joy and less interest in things that brought pleasure to a person.
- Events in life, such as bereavement, cause mood changes that can typically be differentiated from depression characteristics.
- Depression causes are not fully understood but are likely to be a complex mix of genetic, physiological, environmental, and psychosocial factors.

Depression diagnosis is a mood disorder marked by persistently low mood and a sense of depression and loss of interest. It's an ongoing problem, not a passing one, lasting 6 to 8 months on average.

Depression diagnosis begins with a doctor or mental health specialist consultation. To rule out various causes of depression, ensure reliable differential diagnosis, and secure safe and effective care, it is essential to seek the assistance of a health professional.

3.2   How depression is different?

Depression is different from the mood fluctuations experienced by people as part of a healthy life. Depression does not involve transient emotional responses to the problems of everyday life.

Similarly, if it does not linger, even the sensation of sorrow arising from someone close to death is not itself depression. Depression may, however, be related to deprivation-when depression follows a loss, psychologists call it' complicated deprivation.

Signs and symptoms of depression may include:

- Depressed mood
- Reduced interest or pleasure in previously enjoyed activities, loss of sexual desire
- Unintended weight loss (without diet) or low appetite
- Insomnia (difficulty sleeping) or hyper so.

Depression is likely to be due to a complex combination of factors including

- Biology
- Physiological-changes in the rate of neurotransmitters
- Environmental
- Psychological and social (psychosocial)

3.3   Many individuals are at higher risk of depression than others; risk factors include:

Life events: such as grief, divorce, work issues, relationships with family and friends, financial problems

Personality: more vulnerable are those with fewer effective coping strategies or past life trauma.

Genetic factors: first-degree depression relatedness increases the risk. Injury to children:

Many prescription medicines contain corticosteroids, other beta-blockers, interferon, and other prescription medicines.

Recreational drug misuse: alcohol abuse, amphetamine abuse, and other medications are closely associated with depression.

Injury to the anterior neck

Having a major depressive episode: this increases the risk of a subsequent recession.

Chronic pain syndromes: these and other chronic conditions such as diabetes, chronic pulmonary obstructive disease, and cardiovascular disease increase the likelihood of depression.

Treatment medication and therapy may help patient control depression symptoms.

Depression is a mental illness that can be treated.

Depression management has three components:

Get aid from exploring practical solutions and adding pressure to informing family members.

Psychotherapy also referred to as speech therapy, such as cognitive- behavioral therapy (CBT).

Drug treatment, with antidepressants in general:

Psychotherapy The cognitive-behavioral therapy (CBT), relational psychotherapy, and problem-solving counseling are mental and verbal treatments for depression. Psychotherapies are the first treatment option for mild cases of grief; they can be used alongside other medications for moderate or severe incidents.

The two main types of psychotherapy used in depression are?

CBT behavioral therapy

CBT can be administered with a psychologist, face-to-face, in groups, or over

the telephone in individual sessions. Several recent studies suggest that CBT can be implemented effectively through a computer-based relational counseling that helps patients recognize psychological issues that affect relationships and interaction and how they, in turn, affect mood and can be improved.

Antidepressant medicines

Antidepressants are medicines that are available from a doctor on prescription. Drugs are used for moderate to severe depression, but are not recommended for children, and are prescribed to teenagers only with caution. Selective serotonin reuptake inhibitors (SSRIs)

- Monoamine oxidase inhibitors (MAOIs)

- Tricyclic antidepressants

- Atypical antidepressants

- Selective serotonin reuptake inhibitors (SNRIs)

Every type of antidepressant works on a specific neurotransmitter. The medications must proceed as recommended by the doctor to prevent recurrence, even after symptoms have improved.

A Food and Drug Administration (FDA) warns that anti-depressant drugs may increase suicidal thoughts. Any issues should always be discussed with a physician, including any intention to stop taking antidepressants.

Exercise and other therapies Aerobic exercise can help with mild depression because it increases levels of endorphin and activates the mood-related neurotransmitter norepinephrine.

Brain stimulation therapies are also used in anxiety, including electroconvulsive therapy. Repetitive magnetic transcranial stimulation sends magnetic pulses to the brain and can be active in major depressive disorder.

Electroconvulsive therapy severe depression cases that have not responded to drug therapy can benefit from electroconvulsive therapy (ECT); this is especially effective for psychotic depression.

Types Unipolar or bipolar depression

It is considered unipolar depression if the primary characteristic is a depressed mood. Nevertheless, if it is characterized by manic or depressive symptoms separated by periods of healthy atmosphere, it is referred to as bipolar disorder (formerly related to as manic depression).

Anxiety and other signs can include unipolar depression-but no manic episodes. Nevertheless, research shows that people with bipolar disorder are depressed for about 40 percent of the time, making it difficult to differentiate between the two conditions.

Total psychotic depressive disorder this disease is characterized by psychosis-accompanied depression. Psychosis can include delusions — false beliefs and detachment from reality, or hallucinations — sensing things that are not there.

Postpartum depression It is often more severe for women to experience "baby blues" with a child, but postpartum depression-also known as postnatal depression.

Minor seasonal depressive disorder previously called seasonal affective disorder (SAD), this illness is due to the decreased winter sunlight-the depression happens during this season but rises for the remainder of the year and in response to light therapy.

Significant and severe winter countries tend to be more affected by this disease.

While the name may indicate that this is not a severe condition, changes in mood may become more severe, sometimes helping to deal with depression early.

3.4   Symptoms of Mild Depression, How to Get Rid of Depression?

Mild depression symptoms may include feeling hopeless, self-looking, wanting to remain alone, and negative thoughts.

Significant changes in moods and behavior, as well as increased physical sensations, can signify mild depression.

Common symptoms include:

• Irritability

• Suicidal Thoughts

• Feeling Excessively Exhausted

• Feeling Hopeless

• Feeling Extremely Sad

• Being Always On the Verge of Tears

• Self-Loathing

• Having Difficulty Concentrating

• Feeling Unmotivated

• Wanting to Be Left Alone

• Having Unexplained, Mild Aches and Pains You are losing patience with others.

The habits of sleep may change, and appetite may increase or decrease.

People with mild depression, including cigarettes, opioids, and alcohol, may also use more mood enhancers.

Types of depression

As stated by Harvard Medical School, six common types of depression are listed below.

Moderate depression or dysthymia

It is often referred to as chronic depressive disorder. For about two years, a person diagnosed with this condition will have symptoms mentioned above. Usually, they can handle their daily lives, but with little enjoyment or pleasure.

• Major depression can cause extremely dark moods that can lead to thoughts of suicide.

• During the shorter days of fall and winter, seasonal affective disorder is often triggered. This condition can contribute to a lack of sunlight and changing sleep patterns.

• During and after pregnancy, perinatal and postpartum depression can affect people. This may be moderate or extreme depression.

• Premenstrual dysphoric disorder is a severe form of premenstrual syndrome, commonly referred to as PMS.

• Signs of minor or major depression may be associated with bipolar disorder. Furthermore, before or after a period of high energy and activity, these signs are known as depressive or hypomanic.

Moderate depression:

The depression experience can change over time. There may be additional signs, such as dark times and sleeplessness.

Some signs may escalate like Occasional worrying spells can turn into an almost constant negative emphasis. Repeated irritation can become constant frustration with friends.

These types of changes may indicate a shift from moderate to mild depression. If a patient notices any changes in symptoms, a doctor should be consulted.

Severe depression tends to notice severe or major depression. The disorder is excruciating, making the quality of normal activities extremely difficult.

Severe depression is often associated with symptoms similar to milder forms. A person with severe depression, however, may also experience • delusions• hallucinations • self-harm, or suicidal thoughts. A patient with this disorder may need medication, and a psychiatrist might prescribe a form of talk therapy.

The most commonly prescribed treatments for severe depression are selective serotonin reuptake inhibitors (SSRIs). Definitions of SSRIs include:

- Citalopram
- Escitalopram
- Fluoxetine
- Paroxetine
- Sertraline benzodiazepines,

But with repeated usage, they may become addictive. Doctors usually recommend them if there have been no other choices.

A physician can recommend electroconvulsive therapy for severe depression if the many other types of medication and treatment have not been successful. This involves a person under anesthesia receiving an electrical current in the brain. This can be done 2-3 times a week, resulting in 6-12 treatments.

A doctor's visit is often an excellent way to begin dealing with depression. The physician will evaluate the symptoms caused by depression and decide the degree of the disorder.

Most online tests suggest that depression can be detected. Developed in 1999, the PHQ-9 analysis is based on clinical guidelines for diagnosis. It has only nine questions that doctors use to recognize the existence and form of depression in many countries.

Anyone who is unsure of talking to a doctor may find it helpful to take the online PHQ-9 test.

Simple lifestyle changes are often used to combat mild depression. These may involve changing the diet and sleep patterns of an individual or improving the balance between work and life. It can also help to spend time away from television and social media.

Changes in lifestyle can help other people find their interests can help with mild depression. A recent study suggested that people who took on creative pastimes "had more positive and less negative mood, more interest, less stress, and lower heart rate when engaging in leisure than when not." Busy lifestyles lend themselves to shortcuts, which may involve the use of time- saving devices, means of transport, or meals. These may be beneficial, but may also restrict healthy activities from people.

3.5   Daily Recommendations for Helping with Depression Often Include

- Getting fresh air
- Exercising a little more
- Eating fresh food
- Meditating or just sitting still for 10 minutes
- Limiting the time spent on the computer or watching television, especially at night
- Doing someone a favor

It may be impossible to try some of these tips because of health problems, age, or other faculties. Certain options for treatment are listed below.

Traumatic events may lead to mild depression. If this is the case, and a doctor may recommend a talk therapy when mild depression becomes severe.

Many forms of talk therapy include:

Counseling

A series of sessions may help identify causes of depression with a professional therapist. Counselors do not advise individuals, but they propose that certain aspects of life can be modified.

Interpersonal therapy (IPT)

Many find it difficult to communicate with others, which can lead to loneliness and depression. IPT is intended to help promote relationships.

Psychodynamic therapy

This involves a therapist asking someone to say what's in their mind while the therapist attempts to identify problematic patterns of thinking or behavior. An individual may not be aware of the fact that these patterns cause distress and lead to depression.

Cognitive-behavioral therapy (CBT)

It can offer practical ways to deal with results rather than focusing on the causes of depression. This may include distracting the mind from intrusive thoughts and recognizing signs of a shifting mood from early warning.

CBT is a popular choice because, within weeks, people often see improvement, and therapy tends to require a short-term commitment.

3.6   Who is going to get depression?
According to the World Health Organization, depression was the world's leading cause of Trusted Source of ill health and disability in 2017. Depression can be as common as it does not have a single purpose.

Women are more likely than men to become discouraged. There are different opinions as to why this is the case. The frequent periods for signs to occur are puberty, pregnancy, and menstruation.

Statistics vary from country to country, but depression is more prevalent in the following groups

- Economically disadvantaged people
- People with chronic health conditions, such as coronary heart disease or cancer
- Children of depressed parents
- People with other mental health conditions, such as anxiety.

If a patient is uncertain if medication is associated with emotional changes, a doctor should be consulted.

Outlook

It may be beneficial to recognize depression at an early stage. If a person is unsure of despair, seeing a doctor may be a good idea.

When depression is moderate, there may be dominant, lasting benefits from simple changes in lifestyle. Many people may see these benefits quicker than others.

Anyone with moderate to severe depression must remain in contact with a doctor and report any self-harm, suicide, or harm to others.

Chapter 4: Pessimism

4.1   What is Pessimism?

Pessimism, an attitude of hopelessness towards life and existence, combined with a vague general opinion that the universe is governed by pain and evil.

... Depression is the antithesis of optimism, an attitude of general expectation, combined with the belief that good and pleasure are balanced in the universe. A pessimistic example is a person who always assumes that something will fail

There is no question that pessimism will make your life worse, increase your bad moods, and even lead to depression. A pessimist is, of course, at the top of the list of people who are likely to lose hope and become discouraged.

What is the cause of pessimism?

Why would anyone expect the worse at all times?

The following are some possible psychological reasons for pessimism:

1)   **Poor past experience:** if a person failed enough times, he might start to assume that it is not possible to succeed and thus become pessimistic. I don't say all depressed people don't realize, but pessimism certainly holds back many people and prevents them from achieving.

2)   **Poor company and pessimism:** I'm sure you've met at least one pessimist who never failed because he never tried

anything! Not only is pessimism caused by bad past experience, it can also come from listening to people asking you about their bad past experiences. If you are surrounded by pessimists, then you will definitely become one after the other, even if you never struggled before

3)   **Pessimism and the system of beliefs:** Why would two different people struggle, then one of them is pessimistic while the other stays optimistic? This is due to the variations in their system of beliefs. Pessimism can be triggered by the negative restricting values that people acquire in their lives, and therefore one of the better ways of dealing with pessimism is to change the system of beliefs

4)   **Pessimism and religious beliefs: certainly**, people who have certain religious beliefs appear to be more positive than those who have none. Because pessimism is the absence of optimism that you can cope with pessimism by doing anything that can bring back hope

5)   **Pessimism and self-confidence:** no one can claim why pessimistic people lack confidence, but it is a fact that some people are pessimistic because of lack of self-confidence. If someone has self-doubts or is not sure about his ability to succeed, he will undoubtedly become a pessimist coping with pessimism and pessimism. Whether you are a pessimist or if you come into contact with a pessimistic person who is important to you on a regular basis below are some tips that will help you deal with pessimism: repair your belief system:

6)   **Truth about Success:** from the first attempt, no successful person has ever made it, and even those who excel have experienced several challenges in their lives. Being rational is one of the easiest ways to deal with pessimism.

Many pessimistic people claim to be pessimistic because they are realistic, while in fact if they were realistic, they would have understood that success never happens before failures are encountered Build self-esteem: yes if the cause of your pessimism was low self- esteem, then the best way to deal with it is to build your self-confidence.

4.2   Pessimism means lack of hope or confidence in the future.

Studies suggest that pessimistic people are vulnerable to physical and mental disorders and are susceptible to chronic pain and disease.

A Mayo Clinic research also suggests that people who have developed a positive view of life have a lower incidence of illness than their cynical peers. Here are some of the pessimism's adverse effects:

1.   Depression and other mental and emotional disorders can be triggered.

Pessimism's consequences are far higher than negative outlook growth and lack of hope because it can cause depression. The recurring feeling that things are going wrong or that nothing positive is ever going to happen could cause suicidal thoughts, which can lead to more severe problems such as chronic pain, frustration, insomnia, poor diet, and other mental and emotional issues.

2.   It can lead individuals to neglect their health.

Pessimism can also trigger health problems apart from depression and other emotional issues. This is because people who are cynical appear to be ignorant of their health and do not think much about their situation.

Some of the signs of pessimism include heart problems, diabetes, obesity, high cholesterol, cigarettes, and lack of physical activity. Those with definite opinions, on the other hand, are better educated in better physical, emotional, and mental health and hold stable jobs. This is because they are taking care of themselves, exercising, trying to stay healthy, and trusting in the future.

3.   It can lead people in life to make poor choices.

Pessimistic people rarely make decisions in their lives, and if they do, they typically don't care about the future because they don't believe things will turn out right first.

It's one of the reasons they're less concerned about their health, so they engage in unhealthy habits such as cigarettes, drinking, eating unhealthy foods, and leading sedentary lives. All of these can lead to their declining wellbeing, which is, first and foremost, what they expect.

4.3   Why are some people very pessimistic?

Life disappointments

As a result of so many disappointments, many people become cynical. Generally, these people expect to continue their suffering and their future to be an extension of their history.

Building up negative beliefs

Our ideas come from our convictions. An individual tends to think negatively as negative attitudes build up and assume that the worse will happen. A pessimistic belief in a certain area of life can contribute to pessimism in the same area of life.

Genetics vs. environmental conditions

Some studies say that because of some genes, some people are born pessimists. If a person has some genes, however, they usually don't work before the person passes through some experiences.

Negative programming

Press, friends, and family may be able to program a person to behave in some way. Because a person's way of thinking can change because of the way messages are repeated over and over, and he can become a pessimist.

Anxiety and anxiety causing pessimism

A person who is always worried and anxious can continue to develop negative scenarios in his mind. Because that person is too frightened of something, he continues to picture it in his mind over and over.

Depression causes pessimism

A person who becomes depressed loses hope when he gets what he wants. He becomes very negative when a person loses faith because he can hardly think of any hopeful outcomes (see why people get depressed).

Optimism is influenced by religious beliefs

Many religions promote optimism. A person who believes in a faith that asks him to expect the best is more likely to be positive than a person who follows no religion, assuming there are no other discrepancies between them.

Negativity is contagious

People are negatively infecting each other. Studies have found that even for a short period of time, people who see their friends ' negative status on social networks are likely to think negatively. Pessimism may arise from the fact that pessimistic people are surrounded.

Low self-esteem

While some people with high self-esteem are pessimistic, low self-esteem makes a person think he can't accomplish his goals and, as a result, become pessimistic. The more a person believes in himself, the more he becomes positive (see How to develop self-esteem).

Collecting the wrong experience

Every person interprets in a different way the events that happen to him. A person can make so many negative conclusions about life by giving false meanings to so many games, and thus assume that the worst will always happen.

Guilt

It may lead to pessimism. If a person believes that he is not useful or deserves punishment, he may expect that bad things will happen to him. It is not unusual for a person to think that for his evil deeds, Karma will come after him.

Self-protection

The desire for self-protection may be at the root of pessimism. If a person is too afraid to try something, he may be cynical to prevent himself from ever doing it. A person's subconscious mind usually uses this trick to keep him from his fears.

4.4 Signs You May Be a Pessimist (And How to Fix It)?

You Discredit Victory

It's no wonder that their view of the world is the most significant difference between optimists and pessimists. The optimist will take credit when something good happens, realizing that they are in control of their actions and are responsible for the good things in their lives. We find it a miracle, though, when something good happens to a pessimist. Their actions and intentions do not necessarily correlate with the result.

The founder of Learned Optimism and a pioneer in positive psychology, Martin E. P. Seligman, Ph.D., discovered that how an individual expresses their small accomplishments directly correlate with their overall success in life. Expecting positive results from your decisions will result in better results than expected while assuming adverse outcomes or describing positive outcomes as a fluke will impede development.

The Fix:

Learn from your successes and failures as there are lessons in both – and be grateful for all of them

You Give Up Early

If confronted, pessimists tend to give up and move on while optimists continue to try and solve the problems. For one experiment, optimists and pessimists are assigned the task of solving an anagram, resulting in 50 to 100 percent longer optimists working on the answer.

Persistence is often an indication of the success of the individual. The desire to strive to overcome hardship problems can mean more student achievement, better jobs, cleaner bodies, and happier families.

The Fix

Start the strategy of "fake it to you makes it" and don't give up on the first sign of trouble. Set a goal to keep going for another day if you feel like giving up. Try something new then and see how you feel.

You Find It Difficult To Forgive

It's difficult for a pessimist to forgive. Instead, we are dwelling on problems, grudging, and refusing to let it go. A pessimist not only quickly gives up, but he also gives up in his relationships.

Holding onto another person's perceived wrongs gives the feeling of power to a pessimist. The optimist, on the other hand, feels the need to compromise on disagreements and feels less in charge in conflict situations.

The Fix

Stop holding on to your grudges and let go. Have hard conversations, consider the viewpoint of the other person, and forgive. Forgiveness allows you to step forward without rehabilitating old complaints.

You Expect Bad News

You may have heard "expect the worst, but hope for the best." Ok, the pessimist is anticipating the worst and is not hoping for anything. It's hardly shocking to a pessimist when a promotion is skipped over, or a deal falls through.

The optimist is positive because, even in the face of disappointing news, they keep up their expectations, work hard and continue to expect good things to happen.

The Fix

Rather than hoping for the worst, choosing to hope for the best

You Display Selfish Behavior

Rarely do the pessimist care about others and reflect on their desires and problems.

A pessimist is all about other people's mistakes, while an optimist accepts responsibility for his part and shares the credit.

It's hard to be on a pessimistic team because they always look at how the actions will benefit or hurt them, and they don't look at the bigger picture. An optimist knows that everybody will have a positive experience with a successful team. Even though they disagree with an event, the team's overall performance is more critical.

The Fix:

Start doing random acts of kindness without any motive for parents, friends, and colleagues. Consider the action about them all and leave out your feelings.

You Are Overly Suspicious Of People

It's difficult for cynical people to believe the good that happens to others because of the actions of the other man. Instead, they choose to assume that other people's success is due to their connections or some shady dealings.

This is just the way the pessimist describes why in their lives; they don't see the same success.

The Fix

Instead of discounting the success of somebody, try to ask them about it. To help you achieve your goals, look for strategies that you can implement.

You Are Jealous of Other People's Success

Pessimists, somewhat close to being cynical, are also jealous of the achievements of other people. Criticizing or discounting the happy life of other people as not possible or even made up is easy.

It's a very competitive world, and it's easy to be jealous of the life of someone else, mainly when it's posted on social media.

In fact, there is a direct correlation between envy and the amount of time spent on social media, according to one report.

The Fix:

Stop thinking about everything you're doing and start looking at what makes you happy in your life. Accept life for what it is for other people – their life, and begin to create your happy life.

Chapter 5: Stress

5.1   What is Stress and How to Deal with Stress?

Stress is the way the body reacts to any demand or threat. If you feel danger whether real or imagined, the defenses of the body kick into high gear in a

fast, automatic cycle known as the "fight-or-flight" reaction or the "stress response." The answer to pressure is the way the body protects you. This helps you stay focused, enthusiastic, and alert while working correctly. Stress can save your life in emergency situations giving you extra strength, for example, to defend yourself, or spurring you to slam on the brakes to avoid a car crash.

Stress can help you tackle obstacles as well. It's what keeps you on your toes during a workplace presentation, sharpens your concentration when you try the game-winning free throw or drives you to study for an examination when you'd rather watch television. But beyond a level, pressure stops being helpful and starts to cause serious damage to your health, attitude, performance, relationships, and quality of life.

The effects of chronic stress

When distinguishing between emotional and physical risks, the nervous system is not very strong. If you are over-stressed by an argument with a friend, a job deadline, or a bill hill, your body will respond just as strongly as if you are facing a real life-or-death scenario. And the more you activate your emergency stress system, the easier it gets to trigger, making it more difficult to shut down.

When you appear to get stressed out often, like many of us in the stressful world of today, your body may, most of the time, be in a heightened state of stress. And that can lead to severe health issues. Chronic stress disrupts almost all of the body's processes. It can weaken your immune system, upset your digestive and reproductive systems, increase heart attack and stroke risk, and accelerate the aging process. It can even rewire the brain, making you more vulnerable to anxiety, depression, and other problems of mental health. Health problems caused or exacerbated by stress include:

- Depression and anxiety
- Sleep problems of any kind
- Autoimmune diseases
- Digestive issues
- Skin conditions such as eczema
- Heart disease
- Weight problems
- Reproductive issues
- Learning and memory problems

Signs and symptoms of stress overload

How easily it can crawl on you is the most dangerous thing about stress. You're getting used to that. It's beginning to feel familiar, even healthy. Even as it takes a heavy toll, you don't know how much it affects you. That's why the typical warning signs and symptoms of stress overload are essential to be aware of.

Cognitive symptoms:

- Memory problems
- Inability to concentrate
- Poor judgment
- Seeing only the negative
- Anxious or racing thoughts
- Constant worrying

Emotional symptoms:

Depression or general unhappiness Anxiety and agitation

Moodiness, irritability, or anger Feeling overwhelmed Loneliness and isolation

Other mental or emotional health problems

Physical symptoms:

- Aches and pains
- Diarrhea or constipation
- Nausea, dizziness
- Chest pain, rapid heart rate
- Loss of sex drive
- Frequent colds or flu
-

Behavioral symptoms:

- Eating more or less
- Sleeping too much or too little

- Withdrawing from others
- Procrastinating or neglecting responsibilities
- Using alcohol, cigarettes, or drugs to relax
- Nervous habits (e.g., nail-biting, pacing)

5.2 Causes of stress

Stress-causing situations and pressures are known as stressors. We usually think of stressors as being negative, such as an exhausting work schedule or a rocky relationship. It can be stressful, however, anything that places high demands on you. This includes actual events like getting married, buying a house, going to college, or getting promoted.

Not all stress is due to external factors, of course. Pressure can also be internal or self-generated, when you worry excessively about something that may or may not happen, or have irrational, pessimistic thoughts about life.

Finally, what induces pressure depends on your understanding of it, at least in part. Somebody else may not be doing something that is upsetting for you; they may even enjoy it. While some of us are terrified of getting up in front of people to perform or speak, for example, others live for the spotlight. When one person thrives under pressure and performs best in the face of a tight deadline, another will be shut down as demands for work escalate. And while you may enjoy helping care for your elderly parents, your siblings may be overwhelming and stressful in finding care demands.

Common external causes of stress include:

- Major life changes
- Work or school
- Relationship difficulties
- Financial problem
- Being too busy
- Children and family

Common internal causes of stress include:

- Pessimism
- Inability to accept uncertainty
- Rigid thinking, lack of flexibility
- Negative self-talk
- Unrealistic expectations / perfectionism
- All-or-nothing attitude

What's stressful for you?

Whatever event or situation is stressing you out; there are ways of coping with the problem and regaining your balance. Some of life's most common sources of stress include:

Stress at work

While some workplace stress is normal, excessive stress can interfere with your productivity and performance, impact your physical and emotional health, and affect your relationships and home life. The difference between success and failure on the job can even be measured. Whatever your ambitions or work demands, there are steps you can take to protect yourself from the damaging effects of stress, improve your job satisfaction, and bolster your well-being in and out of the workplace.

Losing a job and experiencing unemployment

It is one of the most stressful experiences of life. Feeling angry, hurt, or depressed, grieving for all you've lost, or feeling anxious about what the future holds, is normal. Job loss and unemployment involves a lot of change all at once, which can rock your sense of purpose and self-esteem. While the stress can seem overwhelming, there are many steps you can take to come out of this difficult period stronger, more resilient, and with a renewed sense of purpose.

Caregiver stress

Caregiver stress may be overwhelming, especially if you think you're in over your head or have little control over the situation. If care pressure continues unchecked, it can take a toll on your wellbeing, relationships, and attitude— eventually leading to burnout. There are plenty of things you can do, however, to rein in the stress of care and to regain a sense of balance, joy, and hope in your life.

Grief and loss

It is one of the greatest stressors in life to cope with the loss of someone or something you love. The pain and loss of stress can often feel overwhelming. You can handle all kinds of emotions that are challenging and unpredictable, from surprise and indignation to disappointment, remorse, and deep sadness. While there is no right or wrong way to grieve, there are healthy ways to cope with the pain that can make your sorrow easier in time and help you deal with your loss, find new meaning, and move on with your life.

How much stress is too much?

Due to the widespread damage that can cause stress, knowing your own limit is crucial. Many people appear to be able to roll with the punches of life, while others seem to collapse when faced with minor challenges or grievances. Some people are even thriving on a high-stress lifestyle excitement.

Factors that affect your level of stress tolerance include:

Your network of support

An enormous shield against pressure is a wide network of supportive friends and family members. The stresses of life do not seem as daunting when you have friends you can rely on. The lonelier and isolated you are on the flip side, the higher the chance of succumbing to pressure.

Your command sense

If you have confidence in yourself and your ability to influence events and persevere with challenges, taking stress in step is easier. On the other hand, when you feel you have little control over your life that you are at the mercy of your surroundings and circumstances stress is more likely to knock you off course.

Your attitude and perspective

The way you look at life and the unavoidable obstacles it poses make a huge difference in your ability to deal with stress. If you are generally optimistic and hopeful, you will be less vulnerable. Stress-hard people tend to embrace challenges, feel more positive, believe in a higher purpose, and accept change as an inevitable part of life.

Your ability to handle your emotions

If you don't know how to calm down and calm down when you feel sad, angry, or troubled, you are more likely to get stressed and agitated. Having the ability to identify and cope with your feelings properly will increase your stress tolerance and help you heal from adversity.

Your planning and awareness

The more you are conscious of a stressful situation, including how long and what to expect, the easier it is to deal with. For example, if you go into surgery with a realistic picture of what to expect after surgery, a painful recovery will be less stressful than if you expected to bounce back immediately.

5.3 Improving your Ability to Handle Stress

Get on the move. One strategy you can use right now to help relieve pressure and start feeling good is to increase your activity level. Regular exercise will lift your mood and relieve you from stress, allowing you to break out of the loop of negative thoughts that fuel stress. Rhythmic exercises like walking, running, swimming, and dancing are especially effective, especially if you exercise attentively (focusing your attention on the physical sensations you experience as you move).

You are connecting with others. Hormones that relieve stress when you feel irritated or anxious can be caused by the simple act of speaking face to face with another person. Even a brief exchange of kind words or a polite smile from another human being can help calm your nervous system down and soothe it. So, spend time with people who are enhancing your attitude and not allowing your obligations to stop you from having a social life. If you have no close relationships, or your links are the source of stress, make developing deeper and more rewarding connections a priority.

Commit the senses. Another quick way to relieve stress is to engage one or more of your senses view, sound, taste, smell, touch, or motion. The key is finding the feedback of the sensory, which works for you. Would you feel calm by listening to an uplifting song? Or do you smell coffee from the ground? Or maybe it works quickly to pet an animal to make you feel centered? Everybody responds a bit differently to the sensory input, so try to find out what works best for you.

Know relaxation. You can't remove stress from your life completely, but you can control how much it affects you. Relaxation techniques such as yoga, meditation, and deep breathing stimulate the body's response to relaxation, which is the polar opposite of the response to stress. Such practices can reduce your everyday stress levels and improve feelings of happiness and serenity if done regularly. We also improve your capacity under pressure to stay calm and collected.

Eat a good diet. The food you eat can make your mood better or worse and affect your ability to cope with the stressors of life. Eating a diet full of processed and fast foods, refined carbohydrates, and sugary snacks could intensify stress symptoms, while a diet rich in fresh fruit and vegetables, high-quality protein, and omega-3 fatty acids will help you cope better with life ups and downs.

Get the rest of you. Feeling tired can make you think irrationally more stressful. Chronic stress can also interrupt the sleep at the same time. Whether you have trouble sleeping and staying asleep at night, there are many ways to improve your sleep, so you feel less anxious and more successful and emotionally balanced.

5.4 The Effects of Stress on Your Body

You're sitting in traffic, watching the minute's tick away for an important meeting late. Your hypothalamus, a tiny brain control tower, wants to deliver the order: send in the hormones of stress! Such stress hormones are the same as those that activate the "fight or flight" response of your body. The races of your heart, your breath, and your muscles are ready for action. This response was designed by preparing you to react quickly to protect your body in an emergency. But if the answer to stress continues to fir, it could put your health at serious risk day after day.

Stress is a natural mental and physical reaction to experiences of life. From time to time, everyone experiences pressure. Anything that can cause pressure from daily responsibilities such as work and family to serious life events such as a new diagnosis, battle, or a loved one's death. Stress can be beneficial for your health for immediate, short-term situations. It can help you deal with circumstances that are potentially serious. By releasing hormones that increase your heart and breathing rates and prepare your muscles to respond, your body responds to stress.

However, if your response to stress does not stop firing, and these levels of stress remain elevated much longer than is necessary for survival, your health may be subject to a toll. Chronic stress can cause symptoms of various kinds and affect your overall well-being.

Chronic stress symptoms include:

- Irritability
- Anxiety
- Depression
- Headaches
- Insomnia

Central nervous and endocrine systems

Your central nervous system (CNS) is responsible for your response to "fight or flight." The hypothalamus gets the ball rolling in your brain, telling your adrenal glands to release adrenaline and cortisol from the stress hormones. Such hormones restore your heartbeat and send racing blood to areas that most need it in an emergency, like your muscles, lungs, and other vital organs.

The hypothalamus must tell all processes to go back to normal when the perceived anxiety is gone. The response will continue if the CNS fails to return to normal, or if the stressor does not go away.

Respiratory and cardiovascular systems

Stress hormones affect your cardiovascular and respiratory systems. You breathe faster during the stress response in an effort to distribute oxygen-rich blood to your body quickly. Stress can make breathing even harder if you already have a breathing problem like asthma or emphysema.

The heart is also beating faster under pressure. Stress hormones cause your blood vessels to constrict and divert more oxygen into your muscles so you will have more power to act. But this also increases the pressure on your blood.

Digestive system

The liver produces extra blood sugar (glucose) under pressure to give you an energy boost. You may not be able to keep up with this extra glucose rush if you are under chronic stress. Chronic stress can increase the risk of type 2 diabetes.

Hormone rushes, fast breathing, and higher heart rate may also upset your digestive system. Due to an increase in stomach acid, you are more likely to have heartburn and acid reflux. Stress does not cause ulcers (often a bacterium named H. pylori does), but it can increase your risk to them and contribute to the development of existing ulcers.

Stress can also influence the flow of food through your body, resulting in diarrhea and constipation. You may also have nausea, diarrhea, and stomach ache.

Muscular system

When you're nervous, the muscles tense up to protect themselves against injury. Once you relax, they tend to release again, but if you are under constant stress, your muscles may not be able to relax. Tight muscles are responsible for headaches, back and shoulder pain, and body aches. This can set off an unhealthy process over time as you stop exercising and turn to relieving pain medication.

Sexuality and reproductive system

For both the body and the mind, stress is exhausting. When you are under constant stress, it's not unusual to lose your desire. Although short-term stress can cause more male hormone testosterone to be released by men, this effect is not lasting.

When pressure lasts for a long time, the levels of testosterone in a person may start to drop. This can affect the production of sperm and cause erectile dysfunction or impotence. Chronic stress can also increase the risk of male reproductive organs such as the prostate and testes

Immune system

Stress stimulates the immune system, which for instant situations can be a plus. Such relaxation will help prevent infections and heal wounds. But over time, your immune system will be weakened by stress hormones and the response of your body to foreign invaders. People under chronic stress, as well as other infections, are more susceptible to viral diseases such as flu and common cold. Stress can also increase the amount of time you need to heal from a disease or injury.

Chapter 6: How to become Optimistic?

6.1.   Here are some ways to become optimistic

Positive thinking brings many benefits with it, such as better wellbeing and better sleep.

Check out theseways to become an optimist and start taking advantage of these advantages.

1.   Create some Positive Mantras:

While most of us believe that our happiness or lack of it is focused on external things, we are often the ones that hold back. Many of us spend our days relying on negative messages that we may not even be aware of, telling ourselves that we are "not good enough," "not smart enough" or "not beautiful enough." You need to change these messages and start thinking more positively. Try to look for your head's negative thoughts and replace them with positive messages. Takedown and repeat these motivating mantras daily.

2.   Focus on Your Success:

Many of us are happy to acknowledge the successes and achievements of other people; however, when it comes to our own, we often play them down or completely ignore them. So start thinking about yourself more positively, you need to remind yourself regularly of what you have and what you can accomplish. Stop listening to your inner negativity, reflect on your past accomplishments, and begin to appreciate your success and what you have to offer.

3. Get A Role Model:

It can help you find a positive role model if you want to be an optimist. Whether you're a colleague, close friend, or even a celebrity, think of the most unflattering, cheerful person you can have. Experiment with the next couple of weeks and try to walk in their shoes. If negativity starts to creep in or you find yourself in a difficult situation, think: "What (insert optimist's name) would you do?" Honestly respond, then try to follow suit.

4. Focus on the Positive:

It's important to remember that it's not things that make us sad, it's our perception and reaction to them, and while you're not always able to change events, you can change your response. Seek to reframe them when negative situations occur by concentrating on the positive or what you learn from the situation. You gained inner strength and resilience, grown closer to a friend through sharing your heartbreak, or learned about yourself. Always try to focus on what you have learned and gained from your experience rather than what you lost.

5. Don't try to predict the future:

When things don't go perfectly in life, optimists prefer to see each case as an isolated event, whereas pessimists always search for bad luck trends and assume "if it happens once, it's going to happen again." It is important, however, to predict the future based on what has already happened. Remember that failing a plan or relationship doesn't make you a failure, and just because something disappointing happened once (or more) doesn't mean it's going to happen again.

6.   Surround Yourself with Positivity:

Spending time with negative people who are constantly seeing the bad in every situation is a sure-fire way to keep you feeling negative as well. To help you stay optimistic, you need to surround yourself with positive people who help you see the good in circumstances and in life in general. This also applies to other life influences such as music, literature, and movies surround yourself with positive influences and see how it affects your mind.

7.   Keep A Diary of Gratitude:

It never fails to escape our notice when something negative happens. The alarm clock does not go off, or your car does not start, leaving you for the rest of the day in a foul mood. How often do you stop and notice that your alarm clock has gone off all those times or that your car has started? Shift your attention and mindset, make a concerted effort to start talking about all the things that are going right and try to be positive, you need to be happy with keeping a journal of gratitude every morning or night, listing all the things you need to be grateful for that day.

8.   Challenge Negative Thoughts:

Most of our negative thoughts focus on our fears, doubts, and low self- esteem. You need to constantly challenge your negative thoughts in order to help you conquer them. Next time you start feeling pessimistic, write down your feelings, and write down your reasons for and against these emotions. Tell yourself, what is the proof that these thoughts are true? What's the proof they're not? You might even try to act consciously the opposite of how you feel and see what is going on. You may find that after all, your pessimistic predictions don't come true.

9.   Focus on solution rather than the problem:

Focus on the solution rather than the problem: pessimists prefer to concentrate on issues whereas optimists are looking for solutions. Although focusing on your issues or disappointments is tempting, note that this won't change your situation. The situation may not feel great, and it may not seem fair, but what happened, whether you like it or not, has happened. Instead of dwelling on what might have been going on, let go of regrets and negative thoughts, get positive, and start planning where you can go.

10.   Fake It:

Optimism doesn't come naturally to us all, and you might find it takes time to change your mind set. While seek to prioritize the move and create a more positive outlook. Studies have found that by going through the physical motions, you can trick yourself into feeling better. So try smiling and laughing more and speaking in a more positive tone instead of going with your instinct. Acting the way, you want to feel is going to help you become an optimist on your way.

11.   Don't dwell on the past:

It's gone, and the most important thing is how you deal with the aftermath. There's no point in taking the blame, whether on your own or on others. You have the ability to change a situation and move forward. It's so easy to say, with the benefit of hindsight,' I should have done things differently.' When bad things have happened, though, look tomorrow as just what it a new day in which good things can happen when you allow them to happen.

6.2.   How to train your mind to be more optimistic?

Even in difficult situations, do you prefer to see the optimistic? Or do you believe the worst right away and focus on the negative?

Some of us fall into one of two groups when it comes to how we view the world:

Positive or negative: And whatever group you fall under, according to experts, has a lot to do with your upbringing.

"Optimism is both a characteristic of personality and a consequence of our climate, a licensed psychotherapist, from my experience. "Babies and children in their homes have picked up the emotional vibes from an early age. If the environment is calm and caring, even if they innately appear to be nervous, children will blossom. But if the home environment is full of chaos and stress, hope is one of the first things to go. It's hard to be emotionally open and optimistic when your parents don't model that for you. "But if you accept yourself as someone who tends to focus on the negative, your upbringing isn't entirely at fault.

"By definition, some people are hopeful, but many of us are now practicing optimism. Anyone can learn to be optimistic the key is to find purpose in work and life, "a professor specializing in workplace attentiveness at Stanford. "If we work with purpose or when we live with purpose, we feel more satisfied and better equipped to see the glass ' half full.'" But while one can lift the other, it's not the same thing. And while optimists are usually tied up as those who see only the positive in any situation, experts also say that's not true.

"Positive thinking doesn't mean you're missing the stressors of life. You are only addressing adversity in a more productive way. "Amid unfortunate circumstances, creating an optimistic vision of life helps one to have a complete relational universe. Reduces feelings of sadness, depression, and anxiety, increases lifespan, fosters stronger relationships with others, and provides coping skills in difficult times. Feeling positive helps you to better deal with stressful situations, which decreases the adverse health effects of stress on your body. "However, psychologists argue that the real difference between optimists and pessimists is not in their level of happiness or how they view a situation, but in how they cope.

"Optimism is an attitude that enables people in the most favorable, positive light possible to see the universe, other people, and events. Many people describe this as the' half glass full' attitude "Optimists accept negative events, but they are more likely to avoid blaming themselves for the bad outcome, are inclined to view the situation as temporary and are likely to expect more positive events in the future."

You're Brain on Optimism:

So what exactly happens in the brain when we have a positive or negative reaction?

Research shows that more left-side activity is correlated with positive moods, while more right-side activity is associated with negative emotions, such as being angry or depressed.

The Workers in high-stress jobs, who, on average, tipped to the right in the psychological set-point ratio, are taught carefulness. The findings were promising: they shifted their emotional quotient to the left after two months of training (for three hours each week) and reported feeling less anxious, more energized, and happier.

Looking on the Bright Side's Tangible Health Benefits:

To be more realistic, is it worth the effort and train the brain? Science is saying,' yes.' Research shows that the positive view of the world has some authentic health and efficiency benefits.

It has been shown that optimism provides physical and mental endurance for individuals, even those who have endured extraordinarily traumatic life conditions or medical situations, "Research also indicates that those with an optimistic outlook appear to be more proactive in terms of their wellbeing, have improved cardiovascular health and a stronger immune system, earn higher incomes and have more performance.

"Optimism can be improved by fairly uncomplicated and low-cost approaches— even something as simple as having people write down and think about the best possible results in different areas of their lives, such as jobs and relationships,"

Encouraging the use of these strategies could be an effective way to improve health in the future.

1. ' Putting On' a Positive Lens:

Yes, it's as easy to shift your outlook as thinking happy thoughts consciously.

"For example, if a person says a whole day was ruined because it was dark or rainy outside, I might ask him to focus on what might have been achieved during that time. He will often respond that he ended up relaxing, reading, or cuddling indoors to someone he loves. I advise clients to make an active effort to' put on' neutral lenses as much as possible instead of looking at things in the most negative light possible. This will become effortless after a while, a more natural and hopeful mentality. "Taking it conscious effort not only changes your point of view in the short term, but it can actually train the brain to think more positively. As Davidson's research revealed, the more in a positive light, we consciously reframe scenarios; the more we train our minds to fire circuits in different regions, eventually changing our response to negative experiences.

2.   Take Company You Keep's Note:

We all have mates who are chronic complainers or gossipers. We consider ourselves hopping on the Debby Downer bandwagon after spending a couple of hours with them. It's clear: its infectious negativity.

Fortunately, it can also be contagious for positive emotions. Having a happy partner or a relative or neighbor who lives within a mile seems to increase the likelihood that you will also be satisfied.

That means it's time to introduce to your network some optimists.

"Start noticing daily which you are spending time with. When you continue to connect with people who are hopeful and rooted in life, you will start to be influenced by their positive energy," "the same applies to the time you spend with pessimistic people. The more negativity you spend time, the more hopeless you can feel. "

3.   Turn Off the News:

It's enough to bring anyone's mood in a downward spiral five minutes of the morning news.

"It can be challenging for people to be positive with the news and current media and politics. The truth is that the moment you turn on the news or read the paper, you are likely to be barred with disappointment and a gloomy outlook on the world," "This, however, is an imbalanced view of the world, and I believe people are trying to minimize their use of the news. I typically recommend that you give yourself enough time to learn the story, after which I suggest you turn off the television and instead spend time doing things that help to maintain your wellbeing and a positive outlook. When you feel the need to deal with the current state of political or world affairs, you may want to consider having a healthy discussion with a friend or family member about it; this still helps you to digest the details but can also provide you with a right level of debate and informed views on the media. "

4.   Write in a Journal for a Few Minutes Each day:

At the end of each day, you're going to write down one or two things that they experienced or witnessed during the day that filled them with appreciation, "It's important to remember that this could be anything a cup of coffee that supplied you with happiness, a spontaneous act of kindness by a stranger, or even taking in some fresh air on your morning walk.

5.   Acknowledge What You Can and Cannot Control:

"While some people may not be able to cope with uncertainty, positive people can adapt and thrive. Consider what in the case you can and can't control. "For example, you can't control the fact that you've been fired or laid off if you lose your job. You should monitor whether you are taking steps to find a new job and whether you are taking care of yourself with proper nutrition and sleep. "Practicing sensitivity is a great way to help counteract the urge to ruminate on day-to-day stressors, which is a breeding ground for depression.

"We sometimes ruminate constantly without really concentrating on the task at hand," "If you can learn to be in the present space (allowing other thoughts to enter your brain but then gently pushing them away) without worrying or thinking about past or future, you can find that there is less room for pessimism"

6.   Don't forget to consider the negative:

It's important to remember that trying to be more positive doesn't mean wearing rose-colored glasses. While seeing the positive in the circumstances is good for our mental health, not seeing the negative will discourage you in the long run.

"Optimism can be negative if it holds you locked up in imagination, and you ignore your current reality. You may be hopeful about having a more lucrative job or loving relationship. Still, if you don't deal with the issues that hold you away from those aspirations, you won't be able to achieve what you want," "A mixture of enthusiasm and practical thinking will help people navigate life. Realist thinking doesn't mean never seeing the positive side of life; it doesn't mean anything. It's just a way to support your optimism with the action steps so you can create a positive future instead of being stuck in fantasy.

Chapter 7: Ways and solutions (How to get rid of them?)

7.1   How to deal with depression?

You can feel helpless when you're depressed. You're not. In addition to therapy and medication at times, there's a lot you can do to fight back on your own. All-natural treatments for depression are improving your actions— your physical activity, diet, and even your way of thinking.

Starting right now, these tips will help you feel better.

1.   Get into a routine:

You need a schedule if you're stressed, says Ian Cook, MD. He's a psychologist and founder of UCLA's Depression Treatment and Clinic Program.

Depression could strip away your life's foundation. It's melting into the next day. It can help you get back on track by setting a gentle daily schedule.

2.   Set goals:

You can feel like you can't achieve anything when you're stressed. Which makes the impression for you worse? To push back, set yourself targets on a daily basis.

"Start really small," says Cook. "Make your target something you can be good at, like every other day doing the dishes."

3.   Exercise:

Temporarily increases well-being molecules known as endorphins. It may also have long-term benefits for depressed people. Regular exercise, Cook notes, helps to enable the brain to rewire itself positively.

How much exercise do you need? To get a profit, you don't need to run marathons. It can help to walk a few days a week.

4.   Eat healthy:

A miracle diet that cures depression does not exist. Nonetheless, watching what you eat is a good idea. When depression tends to make you over-eat, it will help you feel better to regulate your diet.

While nothing is conclusive, Cook says there is evidence that foods containing omega-3 fatty acids (such as salmon and tuna) and folic acid (such as spinach and avocado) can help ease depression.

5.   Get enough rest:

Anxiety can make it challenging to get enough eyes shut, and too little sleep can make it worse.

What are you going to do? Start by making a few lifestyle changes. Go to sleep and get up every day at the same time. Try not to snuggle. Take from your bedroom all the distractions no laptop and no TV. You can find that your sleep is improving in time.

6.   Take responsibility:

You may want to withdraw from life when you're stressed and give up your duties at home and work. Don't. Don't. Staying active and getting commitments daily will help you maintain a lifestyle that can help counter depression. You are grounded and given a sense of achievement.

If you're not up for school or work full-time, that's fine. Speak for part-time. If that seems too much, consider working as a volunteer.

7.   Challenge negative thoughts:

There's a lot of work going on in the battle against anxiety shifting what you feel. You're jumping to the worst possible conclusions when you're down.

Using reason as a natural depression treatment the next time you feel bad about yourself. You may feel like no one likes you, but is there any real proof of that? You may feel like the planet's most worthless person, but is that likely? It takes practice, but in time, before they get out of hand, you can beat back those negative thoughts.

8.   Before using supplements, consult with your doctor:

"There is positive evidence for some depression supplements," Cook says. Fish oil, folic acid, and some are included. But we need to do more work before we know for sure. Until starting any supplement, always check with your doctor, particularly if you are already taking medication.

9.   Do something new:

You're in a rut when you're down. Push yourself to do something else. Visit a museum. Pick up and read a used book on a park bench. Volunteer in the kitchen of a soup. Take a class of languages.

"There are chemical shifts in the brain when we push ourselves to do something special," says Cook. "

10.   Try something new:

Changes the levels of dopamine the chemical in the brain associated with satisfaction, relaxation, and learning." Try to have fun: Make time for things you like if you're sad. What if there's nothing more fun? "That's just a depression symptom," says Cook. This way, you have to keep trying.

7.2   How to overcome your anxiety

About 40 million people have an anxiety disorder, ranging from a generalized anxiety disorder (GAD), described as "intense worrying you can't control" to panic attacks, including heart palpitations, trembling, shaking, and/or sweating.

Whether you're feeling moderate or severe anxiety, you should take steps to calm down and soothe yourself instantly. Here are some of the best ones:

1.   Stand up straight:

"When we're nervous, we're shielding our upper body, where our heart and lungs are by hunching over." For immediate relief from stress, stand up, pull back your arms, place your feet equally and far apart, and spread your neck. Then take a deep breath. Combined with deep breathing, this pose helps your body know that right now, it's not in danger and that it's in control (not helpless). When you can't stand up, pull back your shoulders, and lift your arms. Stop hunching and breathing deeply is the most important thing.

2.   Play the game 5-5-5:

You're always stuck in a (negative) thought loop when you're nervous. Play this to get back to your body and quickly stop your anxiety:

1.   *Look around and list five objects that you can see.*

2.   *List 5 sounds that you can listen to.*

3.   You can feel 5 parts of your body (i.e., rotate your ankle, wiggle your ears, nod up and down your head). It may sound stupid, but it works.

3.   Sniff lavender oil:

There are a lot of healing properties of lavender oil. This fosters a sense of calmness and encourages warm, restful sleep. Headaches can even improve. Keep a bottle of lavender oil at your desk (or in your pocket if you have one) to help reduce anxiety. If you need a boost of calm, breathe it in and rub it in your temples. Bonus points to mix long, even breaths, sniffing.

4.   Watch a funny video:

Yes, that's wrong. Watching your favorite comedian or blooper reel video will allow you to stop feeling anxious quickly. What's the reason? You cannot smile and remain nervous, physiologically. The body relaxes in a way that gets rid of tension after a bout of laughter. Plus, laughter brings in oxygen-rich air that stimulates the heart and lungs and spikes your endorphins, according to the Mayo Clinic.

5.   Go on a brisk walk:

Exercise is a long-established way of reducing anxiety. In addition to improving the rate of feel-good neurotransmitters, a quick walk clears the mind and gives you a deeper breath and depression is closely linked to shallow breathing.

Studies also show that people who regularly exercise consistently are 25% less likely to develop an anxiety disorder.

6.   Consider your anxiety:

This may sound counterintuitive, but Chan sky claims it will actually help you feel less depressed to consider your anxiety (instead of feeling ashamed or irritated by it).

If you inherited your family's depression or your lifestyle, or both, it doesn't matter. Its here now and knowing that you're able to learn how to handle it instead of battling it. Acceptance of this does not mean either giving up. Instead of knowing what works for you when it comes to self-reassuring, it means you stop spending time berating yourself for being nervous.

7.   Listen to the world's most soothing song:

This track was specifically designed to ease the nervous system. It was found that depression was decreased by up to 65%. Here is a repeat loop of it.

8.   Re-label what's going on:

If you're having a panic attack or your heart is pounding, you could easily believe something like, "I'm going to die." Re-label it instead of giving in to this false thinking. Remember: "This is a panic attack. I've had them before, and they're not actually killing me; they're going to go by. That's going to happen eventually, and there's nothing I need to do." Really, panic attacks are an amplification of the body's fight-or-flight response that doesn't destroy you it keeps you alive

9.   Do something:

Clear off your desk a few things. Go to the kitchenette and get a glass of water for yourself. Walkout and find a good flower it doesn't matter. Doing an action breaks the habit of thought, which often starts with anxiety.

7.3   Ways to Free Your Mind Immediately

Sometimes you may have thoughts you tend not to have, such as recurrent fears, minor niggles, or ongoing problems that don't go away. Also, the more intense they are, the more you try to free your mind from these feelings. Try not to think of a big pink elephant, for starters. The more chances you concentrate on not thinking about the elephant, the more your mind will focus on that picture. This is because in dwelling on "not doing" anything, the mind is not healthy. The easiest way to free your mind from distracting and unwanted thoughts is to engage it with other thoughts and suppressor overcomes the source of your thoughts. There are ways you can completely free your mind:

1.   Forgive:

Forgiving another person (or yourself) will help you move forward from the past and get rid of negative emotions and thoughts.

2.   Meditate:

For thousands of years, meditation has been used to clear and relax the mind. Doing so doesn't have to include burning candles and sitting in the lotus position; it can just sit comfortably, allowing thoughts to enter your mind and move through without getting involved in them. It can be enough to free your mind from repetitive or distracting thoughts for as little as ten minutes.

3.   Workout:

The workout focuses the body on its physical needs and deprives the brain of your energy. Exercise often releases endorphins and reduces cortisol, which often leads to a more positive and happier mood.

4.   Letting go of the past:

Letting go of the past helps you to concentrate on the here and now, as well as helping you choose more positive thoughts.

5.   Be aware:

The practice of keeping your attention on daily actions that you might usually do on autopilot is to be conscious. The brain focuses on the task at hand by exercising mindfulness rather than thoughts and feelings that you might choose not to have.

6.   Emotional Freedom Technique (EFT):

It is something you can learn quickly (in a matter of minutes) and help you feel better right away. EFT is also often referred to as taping. EFT involves verbalizing the issue or problem in hand while using a term of reinforcement or pressing energy points on the body.

7.   Stop feeling guilty:

Guilt is an emotion that can intensify and leave you helpless and powerless if left unchecked. Note if you feel guilty and find ways to let go of feelings of guilt.

8.   Smile and laugh:

Research shows you're going to feel happier to smile and laugh, even if you don't like it! As you smile, your brain senses the muscle movements in your face and releases hormones and chemicals that make you feel good. The improved feelings will make the way you think easier to adjust.

9.   Watch a funny movie:

Watching a funny film is a good way to get away from reality! Just taking the time to immerse yourself through a movie in another world is often enough to interrupt the over-thinking process.

10.   Avoid people-friendly and approval-seeking habits:

Most people are people-pleasers or approval junkies, but eventually engaging in these behaviors makes you feel trapped as if you are living your life for others. Note when you indulge in these habits and start living for you.

11.   Just do it!

Do one thing today that scares you or throws you off. The dopamine that your body produces will put your mind into sharp focus.

12.   De-clutter your physical possessions:

A clutter-free, relaxing atmosphere will help you reach a more comfortable state of mind. You are freer to encourage your mind to concentrate on more positive thoughts without the stress of cluttering around.

13.   Visualize yourself as the person you want to be:

Think of someone you respect and imagine how you're going to handle your thoughts. Then imagine the same way you act.

14.   Decide to let go of toxic relationships and cultivate positive relationships:

Unhealthy relationships can lead to negative thinking and stressful states. It will enrich your life by maintaining positive relationships, filling your mind with more positive thoughts and memories.

**15.	To work towards a vision, do one thing every day:**

Everything starts with the first move. Identify your goal and the changes you need and decide to take that first leap: you will soon be on your way to achieving your goals instead of just worrying about them.

**16.	Seek hypnosis:**

Hypnosis is a validated technique that helps your subconscious emotions to control your thoughts and feelings, unconscious and awake. Hypnotherapy will strengthen your life's problems and solve them, freeing your mind from worries and concerns.

**17.	Note the interests or things that you love so much that you lose time:**

Do this more often than not! Engaging in a pastime that you enjoy helps foster a more reflective and meditative state of mind. This state allows the brain to relax and focus attentively on the task being pursued, removing any thoughts that may occupy your mind.

**18.	Let go of regrets:**

You can write a letter to yourself or make a list to let go of regrets and then burn it or throw it into a river as a ritual of letting go of regrets.

19. Honor yourself:

Your decisions and let go of self-criticism and judgment.

20. Dance

Move your body and let go of what it looks like you feel! It means that your attitude will change and that your mind will be clear. Take lessons in dance. Learn to tango and dance the new line and get your body moving. You're going to age better and feel good.

21. Spend time alone:

Get used to your own company and just enjoy "being" without constant work, entertainment, or being busy for your own sake.

22. Dear try something new:

Try something new, perhaps a new hobby or even a new selection of meal. Mix things up and get away from your normal way of doing things.

22. Daydream:

Allow daily daydream time. That's so good for your soul!

23. Letting go of labels:

Note how existing labels identify you and let them go.

24. Become less attached to:

To what are you tied? There is nothing wrong with enjoying things in life, but when you become addicted, to make you happy, you depend on something external that occupies the mind.

25. Let go of guilt:

Guilt is an intense and all-consuming strong emotion. Look at what you feel guilty about, and see how you can either solve the problems you feel guilty about or be more positive about yourself.

26. Practice gratitude:

Being thankful allows you to live in the present right now and see the opportunities before you.

27. Write inspirational stories:

Learning about inspiring people and events will help you put your thoughts into a different context.

28. Find people like-minded and optimistic:

If you spend time with people who are positive and like-minded, you invest more of your time in the moment rather than over-thinking and comparing yourself.

29. **Dear make a commitment to keep learning:**

Learning makes you broaden your mind, which can help you achieve a more educated and enlightened viewpoint.

30. **Using positive statements:**

You affirm the way you think and talk all the time. "Things never go my way," for instance, is a negative statement. You can substitute such a thought with a positive statement like "things work beautifully out." Use positive statements helps you make better choices and see things from a different and more optimistic point of view.

7.4　How to keep your mind active?

Everyone has the odd "senior moment." Perhaps during a discussion, you went into the kitchen and can't remember why, or can't remember a familiar name. Memory lapses can occur at any age, but usually, aging alone is not a cause of cognitive decline. If severe memory loss occurs in older people, it is not usually caused by age, but by organic diseases, brain injury, or neurological disease.

Research has shown that with some basic good health habits, you could help prevent cognitive decline and reduce the risk of dementia:

- Remain physically active

- Get enough sleep

- Not smoking

- Have good social interactions

- Restricting alcohol to one drink a day

- Eating a balanced diet low in saturated and Tran's fats.

Diabetes, high blood pressure, sleep apnea, anxiety, and hypothyroidism are some health conditions that may impair cognitive abilities. If you have any of these health problems, by closely following the advice of your doctor, you can help protect your memory.

Changes in memory can be stressful, but the good news is that you can learn how to get your brain working, thanks to decades of study. We can use different strategies to preserve and improve memory. Here's a couple you can try.

1.   Keep learning:

Better mental health in old age is associated with a higher level of education. Experts believe that advanced education will help to keep memory intact by bringing a person into a mentally active routine. It is assumed that stimulating the brain with cognitive exercise stimulates pathways that help maintain and promote interaction between individual brain cells. Most people have jobs that keep them mentally active, but it can work the same way and help improve memory by doing a hobby, learning a new skill, or volunteering for a project at work requiring a skill that you normally don't use.

2.   Use all the senses:

The more senses you use to know something, the more you use your mind to preserve your memory. For one experiment, a series of emotionally neutral photographs were shown to adults, each followed by ascent. They've not been asked to remember what they've seen. Earlier, a set of images were shown, this time without odors, and asked to suggest what they had previously seen. For all odor-paired pictures, and particularly for those associated with good smells, they had excellent memories. Brain imaging showed that when people saw items originally associated with odors, the brain's main odor-processing area became involved, although the odors were no longer present, and the participants had not tried to remember them.

3.   Believe in yourself:

Aging theories can lead to a memory that fails. Middle-aged and older students find memory tasks harder when they are subjected to negative stereotypes about aging and memory and stronger when memory maintenance messages are positive in old age. People who believe they are not in charge of their memory function— kidding about "senior moments" too often, maybe are less likely to work to preserve and improve their memory skills and are therefore more likely to experience cognitive decline.

You have a better chance of keeping your mind sharp if you believe you can change and turn the confidence into reality.

4.   Prioritize your brain use

If you don't need to use mental energy to recall where you put your keys or the birthday party of your granddaughter, you'll be abler to focus on learning and understanding new and important things. To keep daily data open, take advantage of calendars and schedules, maps, shopping lists, file folders, and address books. Designate your glasses, wallet, keys, and other things that you often use at home.

5.   Repeat what you want to know:

Say it loudly or write it down when you want to remember something you just learned, read, or thought about. You reinforce the memory or link that way. For example, if someone's name has just been revealed, use it when speaking to him or her: "So, John, where did you meet Camille?"

6.   Stretch it out:

If correctly paced, repetition is most effective as a learning tool. In a short time, it's best not to repeat something many times, as if you were cramming for a test. Alternatively, for increasingly longer periods of time, re-study the fundamental elements — once an hour, then every few hours, then every day. Spacing out study times helps to improve memory and is especially valuable when trying to master complex data, such as the specifics of a new job assignment.

7.5   How to Keep Your Mind Sharpe?

Here are ten things that you can integrate into your life to help keep your mind focused, and your brain fed:

1.   Exercise:

The mind and body have long been understood to be intertwined. What is the value of the mind for the body? To keep the brain safe, regular exercise goes a long way.

2.   Read a book:

Learning on many levels is helpful. Not only do you learn the information contained in the book as you read, but the act of reading itself generates links within the brain to make it more flexible.

3.   Eat Right:

Most things have been connected to a healthy brain, including nuts, fish, and red wine. Yet focusing on a balanced all-around diet may be the best dietary strategy to keep the mind active.

4.   Maintain good posture:

Maintaining a slouched, upright posture increases circulation and blood flow to the brain.

5. Sleep Well:

For a healthy mind, particularly memory, a good night's sleep is important. Get enough sleep and take naps, if needed.

6. Paint, draw, or doodle:

Whether it's a masterpiece or just a doodle, just making a picture is a great brain exercise.

7. Listen to Music:

Music has a profound effect on the brain and has been correlated with enhanced functioning of intelligence and memory.

8. Learn something new:

For adults, colleges offer entertaining, low-cost seminars and courses. Whether you're learning a new language or improving your computer skills, continuing education is a healthy way to stay sharp.

9. Do Puzzles:

You exercise your brain and increase your mental capacity if you challenge and stimulate yourself mentally. Crosswords are a popular choice, but all kinds of puzzles can be equally helpful. You have to think about how the shapes and colors

match while working jigsaw puzzles. Working puzzles '
problem-solving skills help to keep the mind sharp.

10.   Write:

Reading improves your working memory and communication
skills. It doesn't matter whether it's a family letter, a private
journal, or the "Great American Novel." It's important to know
that although there are no clinically proven strategies to
change the trajectory of brain diseases such as

Alzheimer's, it contributes to a healthy lifestyle which
encourages natural, age-related mental decline, both socially
and mentally. This may reduce the risk of Alzheimer's and
other dementia types.

7.6   How to Overcome Stress in Everyday Life?

You are likely to feel its weight in every area of your life if you
are dealing with a heavy stress load. Stress is normal in
adulthood, but if it is extreme and persistent, it can be
crippling. Fortunately, fear is not only common; it is also
curable. You can overcome stress with the right tools and
return to a happy, healthy life. This article will cover tips for
overcoming anxiety in everyday life; first, in general, we will
go over some background information on stress.

Three main types of stress:

Remember that you're not alone when you feel overcome by
stress. More than 70% of American adults agree that they feel
stressed or are nervous on a daily basis. Such problems are

presented in a variety of forms, but they are general and curable.

It can be helpful to understand the type of stress you are feeling while trying to alleviate stress in your life. Three major types of stress are present: acute, episodic, and chronic. A short-term activity, such as planning a wedding, is responsible for severe stress. Occasional stress is short-term but repeatedly occurs. Meeting work-related deadlines and bringing children to school on time, for example, may cause episodic pressure. On the other hand, chronic stress is long-term stress due to significant life events such as a chronic disease or persistent financial disorder. Each of these types of stress can emerge from all areas of your life, including work, friendships, safety, finance, and trauma, and influence them.

Know that it's normal when you face life stressors and have the physical and mental symptoms that often accompany stress. Luckily, by overcoming the stress, you can relieve your symptoms. More than 50 side effects of stress, including psychological and physical shifts, were described by the American Institute of Stress (AIS). You can lose focus on a mission, feel stressed, have rage spells, have frequent headaches, have trouble sleeping, or experience tense muscles and tiredness.

These are all common signs that will help when you find ways to lower the levels of stress.

When dealing with stress?

It's essential to take care of yourself. It may lead to addictive behaviors such as cigarettes, substance use, and alcohol abuse if you avoid this. Stress could also contribute to drinking, purchasing fuel, overeating, decreased exercise, isolation from social functions, and lower rates of productivity. All of these are common ways to cope with or respond to stress, but they do not solve the stress-induced problem. Instead, things could get worse, and you may find yourself dealing with more severe issues such as anxiety, depression, and acid reflux, other issues related to mental health, heart disease, and stroke. Stress can, of course, cause serious problems.

Fortunately, each and every one of these symptoms can be resolved or avoided by taking steps to overcome your stress.

Live A Stress-Reducing Lifestyle:

Changes in lifestyle will aid in your life to alleviate stress. You are likely to have less stress in your life if you fill your life with healthy habits. To help you reduce stress, you can plan ahead and use the strategies below. We can also motivate you to prevent causes.

Meditation and Deep Breathing:

From the aisles of the grocery store to behind your car's wheel, you can try deep breathing anywhere. You might also want to explore meditation and yoga if this works for you. In general, yoga will relax your back, neck, and chest muscles, all of which are usually influenced by stress.

Exercise:

The pumping of your blood will raise your heart rate and increase your blood pressure. Training also allows the brain to release natural endorphins, helping you to lower stress levels. You're going to want to work out more if you feel better, so a little exercise can kick off a positive cycle quickly.

Get some rest:

If you get enough sleep, reduce your cortisol levels and become more able to cope with everyday tasks. (Cortisol is a stress-related hormone.) If you can't sleep well at night, take a nap. The extra rest of your body may be what it needs to recover from stress.

Physical touch:

A decrease in cortisol levels and lower blood pressure has been shown in physical contact with another human being. Give a kiss to your friend or family member, and admire your significant other's intimacy. For both sides, physical contact would certainly lower stress levels.

Create Structured To-Do Lists:

It can make busy schedules less stressful to plan your days and weeks in advance. You can make sure that you stay productive without overdoing it. They can also use to-dodo lists to help balance time for personal and professional duties. Consider building in time not just for productivity, but also for rest and self-care when you're making plans. Proactively scheduling is a great tool to prevent or eliminate stressors on a daily basis.

Take a shower:

The quiet time alone and the water on your body can significantly reduce stress levels when you take a bath. Add the following essential oils to your bathroom, and aromatherapy will help further reduce your stress: Lavender, Sandalwood, Roman Chamomile, Orange, Rose, and Frankincense. Please remember to feature all genders in photos that being said, we're going to move picture 4 to the section above because it might be challenging to find a picture of a man taking a bath!

Regulate your diet:

Some nutrients can provide stress-fighting fuel for your body. Consider adding green tea to your diet with Omega-3 fatty acids. You may also want to take dietary supplements to reduce stress levels, such as lemon balm, kava- kava, and valerian root. Avoiding caffeine can be an intelligent choice because it can actually exacerbate symptoms by its jitters and crashes.

Finding a Convenient Therapist:

Meeting with a professional counselor will help you reduce anxiety quickly, along with these lifestyle changes. I will teach you how to deal with stress and recognize its patterns, so you can make a difference in your life. You may want to find a convenient option like Better Help if you are already dealing with a busy schedule. Better Help provides years of experience to

licensed counselors, enabling you to access assistance anytime and anywhere. Below you can see reviews of Better Help consultants from people with similar problems

7.7 Anger affects your mental health how it would be controlled?

Anger is a normal feeling, and when it helps you work through issues or problems, whether at work or at home, it can be a positive emotion.

However, if it leads to aggression, outbursts, or even physical altercations, anger can become problematic.

To help you avoid doing or doing something you may regret anger management is necessary. You can use specific strategies to suppress frustration before rage escalates.

There are 25 ways in which you can control your anger:

1.   Count down:

Count down to 10 (or up). Start at 100 if you're really nuts. The heart rate will slow as long as it takes you to count, and the frustration is likely to subside.

2.   Take a breather:

When you get angry, your breathing becomes shallower and speeds up. Reverse this trend (and your anger) by taking slow, deep breaths out of your nose and exhaling for several moments out of your mouth.

3.   Go around:

Exercise Trusted Source can help you calm your nerves and reduce your anger. Go for a walk, hit some golf balls, or ride your bike. Anything that pumps your limbs is right for your body and mind.

4.   Relax your muscles:

Progressive muscle relaxation calls for you to relax, one at a time, in your body, in different muscle groups. Take slow, steady breaths as you tense and release.

5.   Say a mantra:

Find a word or sentence that will allow you to calm down and refocus. Repeat the word to yourself again and again when you're upset. "Relax," "Take it easy and all good examples are," You'll be OK.

6.   Stretch:

Arm rolls and rolls of the neck are good examples of no strenuous yoga-like movements that can help control your body and channel your emotions. No need for fancy equipment.

7.   Escape mentally:

Slide into a quiet room, close your eyes, and visualize yourself in a relaxing scene. In the imaginary scene, focus on details: what color is water? Where high are the mountains? Which sounds like the chirping birds? This can help you find calm in the midst of rage.

8.   Play some tunes:

Let your emotions be carried away by music. Put your ear buds in or slide into your car. Crank up your favorite music and get rid of your rage, bop, or sash.

9.   Stop speaking:

You may be tempted to let the angry words fly when you're steamed, but you're more likely to do harm than good. Just as you did as a kid, imagine that your lips are glued closed. By talking, this moment will give you time to collect your thoughts.

10.   Take a timeout:

Make a break for yourself. Sit away from the rest. You can process events in this quiet time and make your emotions neutral. You might even think that time away from others is so beneficial that you would like to incorporate it into your daily routine.

11.   Take action:

Harness the energy of your rage. Sign a submission. Write an official note. Do somebody else something good. Pour into something that is healthy and productive with your energy and emotions.

12.   Write in your diary:

Maybe you can write what you can't say. Identify how you think and how you would like to react. It can help you to calm down and reassess the events leading up to your emotions by expressing it through the written word.

13.   That's right. Find the most immediate solution:

You may be upset that your child has left a mess once again before going to a friend's visit. Close the door. By taking it out of your mind, you could temporarily stop your frustration. Look in any situation for similar resolutions.

14.   Prevent an outburst:

By rehearsing what you'll do and how you'll handle the problem in the future; the training phase also gives you time to play a number of possible solutions.

15. Imagine a stop sign:

If you're frustrated, the universal stop signal will help you calm down. It's a fast way to help you see the need to interrupt you, your actions, and walk away from the moment.

16. That's wrong. Adjust your routine:

Find a new path if you're frustrated with your long commute to work before you've even had coffee. Consider options that may take longer but ultimately leave you less frustrated.

17. Speak to a friend:

Don't get upset at the cases. Support yourself process what happened by speaking to a trustworthy, supportive friend who might offer a new viewpoint.

18. Laugh:

Nothing is as good as a bad mood. Whether it's playing with your kids, watching stand-up or scrolling memes, spread your anger by looking for ways to laugh.

19. Practice gratitude:

If everything feels wrong, take a moment to focus on what's right. Finding out how many good things you have in your life can help you to neutralize anger and turn the situation around.

20.   Set a timer:

It's probably not the first thing you should say that comes to mind when you're angry. Give yourself a certain amount of time before you answer. Every time you're going to be more relaxed and succinct.

21.   Write a letter:

To the person who made you angry: write a letter or message. Then, erase it. Sometimes, it's all you want to show your feelings in some way, even if it's something you'll never see

.

22.   Imagine forgiving them:

It takes a lot of psychological strength to find the courage to forgive someone who has wronged you. If you can't go that far, at least you can pretend you forgive them, and you're going to feel your anger slipping away.

23.   Empathy practice:

Try walking in the shoes of the other person and seeing the situation from their perspective, you will gain a new perspective and become less frustrated as you tell the story and relive the events as they saw it.

24.   Express your anger:

As long as you handle it properly, it's okay to say how you feel. Ask a trusted friend to help you make a calm response accountable. There are no issues with outbursts, but constructive conversation will help to reduce your pressure and relieve your frustration. It can also avoid future problems.

25.   Find a creative channel:

Turn your anger into something tangible. When you feel angry, try to dream about drawing, gardening, or writing poetry. For creative individuals, emotions are powerful muses. Use yours to relieve frustration.

7.8. How to get rid of pessimistic thoughts?

One of the most important practices I've picked up over the past 10 + years is to stop being cynical and instead think more optimistically and constructively.

It makes life feel lighter, not so hard.

It opens new directions to where you want to go and lets you resolve obstacles more quickly (and often get something good out of them).

You should feel less stressed and more driven to keep taking action and sorry for yourself.

But optimism's strengths are good.

But how are you going to take the habit?

Okay, it may sound a little fuzzy to learn to think in a less negative and more positive way.

I want to break it down into 10 practical tips and smaller habits in this week's article that you can get to use today.

1.   Start replacing the negativity in your environment and life:

What you let in your mind during your regular day will have a big impact on your thinking and feeling.

And start asking what you're going to let in your head.

You can do that by asking yourself: take a piece of paper and or a blank file out of your Smartphone and ask yourself: what can I do this week to spend less time with these three sources?

On your paper or phone, come up with ideas and concrete measures to do that.

When you can't take action to do that with all 3 right now, focus on doing it with just one of the sources.

And then spend the time you have now earned on the most positive outlets so people in your life over the next seven days.

2.   When you're in what seems like a negative situation, figure out what's positive and beneficial about it:

How that individual perceives a failure or challenge in life is one of the biggest differences between an optimist and someone who lets depressive thoughts cloud his mind.

For example, when I stumbled into a negative situation, I felt like giving up and going home.

It felt like it was a permanent place in which I got stuck and that anything I did wouldn't make a big difference anyway. And so my mind was full of negative feelings, and I often beat myself up for whatever I did.

I'm going about things differently these days.

I ask myself questions that will inspire me and help me grow when I find myself in a situation that looks bleak or negative.

Questions such as:

•   How is my best friend or parent going to support me in this situation?

•   What's a good thing about this?

•   What can I learn from that?

• What's one thing I can do the next time differently to get a better result, probably?

3. Work out regularly:

When I have hard time thinking about myself from negative thoughts, a short 20-30-minute free weight workout can help me change my headspace.

It's time well spent because it removes so many internal pressures and anxiety, makes me feel relaxed and happier again.

It's calming my mind, and I'm in a far better place to handle what's going on in my life right now when I'm finished with the workout.

Working out on a regular schedule several times a week also helps me avoid, first of all, getting stuck in a pessimistic funk.

4. Stop mountaineering from a molehill:

This was one of my biggest problems. In my mind, I blew up monsters with small or medium-sized issues or challenges.

Not a good habit if you want to take action to move forward or if in your daily life, you don't want a lot of worries and fear.

In my experience, the easiest way to get grounded in a situation where you begin to feel like you can make a mountain out of a molehill is to zoom out a little on your life using a question like Will this matter happen in five years? Or even for five weeks?

To me, I find the answer is almost always that it's not going, to be honest.

5.   Be thankful for some of the things that you can always take for granted:

If your lens that you see through your daily life is tinted in a negative way, then it's easy to miss the stuff that you can be grateful for.

You have so many, so many things in the world that you don't have or things that you might take for granted.

Take a minute as you get out of bed in the morning or get into it in the evening and focus on a few things like that.

A few of those to which I most often return are

•   Three regular meals a day.

•   A rainy day roof over my head and long, cold seasons here in Sweden.

•   Clean water as much as I want.

•   The warm and happy friends I have in my life.

This one is also a good way to change your attitude if you have a disappointment or loss.

Take a minute or more to think about what you might be grateful for.

6.   Return to this moment (and stay here):

When you're on the train of negative thoughts, you often think of something that happened.

You are going to revive it. Thinking about what you could or should have done or said over and over again.

Or you're thinking of something that might happen.

Or perhaps a combination of the two as a past experience and two will create a nightmare in your mind about what the future could bring.

Snapback into this moment to get out of any of those places right now, what's right here.

If you make this a habit and try to spend more of your day in this present space, then you're going to have fewer negative thoughts and focus more on what's good and what you can do to move forward in this very moment.

And how are you doing this in practice?

A few of my favorite ways to get me back to being attentive and into this moment are:

•   Spend 1-2 minutes just taking in the world around you:

Take a very quick break and just focus 100% on what are around you right now- The colors, the smells. How the sun warms the skin or the feeling of your clothing. The people are walking through your window, and the children's sounds are playing a little further away.

•   Just concentrate on your breathing for 1-2 minutes:

Take a little deeper breath than you normally do. Make sure you breathe through your nostrils and your stomach. Focus on the air coming in and out of you and nothing else during this short break.

7.   Let it go:

If you let your mind ride around with negative thoughts, they will drag you down.

The exercise can help you free them. Or you can use questions as mentioned above to encourage positive thinking.

Another thing that really works well is just letting it out.

Please speak to someone close to you about the negative situation.

Winding up for a few minutes can really help you find a new, more grounded view of the situation. You can figure things out for yourself as the other person listens and what you want to do about it.

Or you might want more active assistance.

If you both have a conversation about the situation, you can find a more helpful perspective together and maybe even the start of an action plan for what you can do to make things better.

8.   Take the positivity to someone else's life:

If you get caught in a negative mentality or victim thought, then one of the simplest ways to get out of that and out of your own head is to take somebody's positivity into your life.

You will feel better about yourself and more optimistic again by adding it and seeing him or her light up and becoming happier.

Here's three ways you can do that:

• Be kind: offer a genuine compliment in music or cooking about her great taste, hold the door, or let someone in your lane while driving your car.

• Help out: offer some good advice that worked well for you in the same situation your friend or colleague is in right now. Perhaps support setting up this weekend's party for your buddy or as he transitions next week to a new apartment.

• Just be there: listen like she's winding. And think about her difficult task and circumstance to help her find her way out.

9. Go slowly:

If I go too fast, if I think, talk and move too quickly, then things don't go well.

Stress builds up and thinking logically and level-headedly becomes more challenging.

Negative thoughts start spinning more often in my head, and it's hard to handle them or bring them to a halt.

If I slow down on the other side, my mind and body will also calm down. Seeing the optimistic perspective and a constructive way forward to what I want is getting easier again.

10.　Get your day off to a positive start:

The first few things you do in the morning always set the tone for your whole day.

If you get off to a negative or gloomy start, then these thoughts or views can be quite difficult to shake.

But if you get the morning off to a positive start, sticking with that feeling and enthusiasm all the way to bedtime becomes much simpler.

A few easy ways to make a positive start to your day are?

•　A quick reminder on your bedside table or bathroom mirror: it might be a quote that really motivated you. And right now, your main priority and vision. Write it down on a piece of paper and put it where you will see when you wake up in the first 1-3 minutes.

•　Get some positive information or conversation that flows into your mind: listen to a podcast or some of your favorite music, read an uplifting blog post or chapter in a book that makes you laugh. Or you can have a fun or inspiring discussion over breakfast with your kids, wife, co-worker, or friend, or as you go to school or work by bus.

•　Twitter or Facebook

7.9   Simple Ways to Relieve Stress and Anxiety Share on Pinterest

Stress and anxiety for most people are common experiences.

In fact, 70% of adults in the United States say they feel stress or anxiety every day.

Here are 16 simple ways of relieving anxiety and stress.

1.   Working out

Is one of the most important things you can do in the fight against pressure? It may seem contradictory, but exercising may alleviate mental stress by imposing physical stress on your body.

When you exercise regularly, the advantages are greatest. People who regularly exercise are less likely to experience depression than those who do not exercise.

There are a few factors behind this:

•   **Stress hormones:** exercise reduces the long-term stress hormones of your body, such as cortisol. It also helps release endorphins, chemicals that enhance your mood and act as natural pain relievers.

•   **Sleep:** exercise can also improve the quality of your sleep that can be adversely affected by stress and anxiety.

- **Trust:** you may feel more competent and confident in your body when you exercise regularly, which in turn promotes mental well-being.

Try to find a routine exercise or activity that you enjoy, such as walking, dancing, climbing, or yoga.

Activities that involve repetitive movements of large muscle groups such as walking or jogging can particularly stress relieving.

➢ **SUMMARY:** By releasing endorphins and improving your sleep and self-image, regular exercise can help reduce stress and anxiety.

2. Consider supplements:

A variety of supplements encourage stress and reduction of anxiety. Here's a brief overview of some of the most common:

- **Lemon balm:** Lemon balm is a mint family member researched for its anti-anxiety effects

- **Omega-3 fatty acids:** One study showed that medical students consuming omega-3 supplements had a 20% reduction in symptoms of anxiety

- **Ashwagandha:** Ashwagandha is an herb used for managing stress and anxiety in Ayurvedic medicine. Several studies suggest it is reliable.

- **Green tea:** Green tea contains many antioxidant polyphenols that are beneficial to health. Through -serotonin levels, it can reduce stress and anxiety.

- **Valerian:** because of its calming influence, Valerian root is a common sleep aid. This contains valerenic acid, which activates the receptors of gamma-aminobutyric acid (GABA) to reduce anxiety.

- **Kava kava:** Kava kava is a pepper family psychoactive member. Often used as a sedative in the South Pacific, moderate stress and depression are gradually being treated in Europe and the US.

Some supplements can interfere with medicines or have side effects, so if you have a medical condition, you may want to speak with a doctor.

Ashwagandha store, omega-3 supplements, digital green tea, and lemon balm.

➤ **SUMMARY:** Many supplements, including ashwagandha, omega-3 fatty acids, and green tea, and lemon balm, can alleviate stress and anxiety.

3.   **The use of essential oils**

The burning of a scented candle can help to reduce the feelings of stress and anxiety.

Some of the fragrances are especially calming. Here are some of the sweetest scents:

- Lavender

- Rose

- Vetiver

- Bergamot

- Roman chamomile

- Neroli

- Frankincense

- Ylang ylang

- Orange or orange blossom

- Geranium Using aromatherapy to treat your mood. Several studies show that depression can be minimized Enhanced by aromatherapy

➤ **SUMMARY:** aromatherapy can help lower anxiety and stress. In order to benefit from calming scents, light a candle, or use essential oils.

4. Reduce your intake of caffeine:

Caffeine is a stimulant found in drinks such as coffee, tea, chocolate, and energy. High doses can increase anxiety. For how much caffeine they can tolerate, people have different thresholds.

Consider cutting back if you find that caffeine makes you jittery or nervous. While many studies show that coffee can be moderately healthy, it is not for everyone. In general, a moderate amount is considered to be five or fewer cups per day.

SUMMARY: High amounts of caffeine can increase anxiety and stress. The sensitivity of people to caffeine, however, can vary greatly.

5. Write It Down:

Writing things down is one way to handle stress.

Although one solution is to document what you're worried about, another is to jot down what you're grateful for.

Gratitude can help alleviate stress and anxiety by focusing your thoughts on the positive aspects of your life.

SUMMARY: Maintaining a newspaper can help relieve stress and anxiety, especially if you focus on the positive.

6. Chew Gum:

Try to chew a stick of gum for a super easy and fast stress reliever.

One study showed that gum chewers had a greater sense of well-being and lower stress. One possible explanation is that gum chewing causes brain waves similar to those of relaxed people. Another is that gum chewing enhances the brain's blood flow.

In fact, one recent study found that stress relief was highest if people chewed more strongly

➤ **SUMMARY:** chewing gum can help you relax, according to several reports. It can also lead to well-being and reduce stress.

7. Spend time with friends and family:

Friends and family social support will help you get through stressful times. Feeling part of a network of friends gives you a sense of belonging and self- worth that can support you in times of difficulty.

One study found that spending time with friends and children, especially for women, helps to release oxytocin, a natural stress reliever. This effect is called "tend and friend," and is the opposite of the fight-or-flight response. Keep in mind that friendship benefits men and women alike.

The study found that men and women with the fewest social connections were more likely to suffer from depression and anxiety

➤ **SUMMARY:** having strong social ties can help you get through stressful times and decrease your anxiety risk.

8. Laugh:

When you laugh, it's hard to feel anxious. It's good for your health, and it can help relieve stress in a few ways:

• Relieving your response to stress.

• Relax your muscles by relieving tension.

Also, laughter can help improve your immune system and mood in the long term.

A research of people with cancer showed more stress relief experienced by people in the humor intervention group than by those who were merely distracted. Try watching a funny TV show or hanging out with friends who make you laugh.

➤ **SUMMARY:** In everyday life, find the humor, spend time with funny friends, and watch a comedy show to help relieve tension.

9. Learn to say no:

Not all stressors are under your control, but some are within your control. Take control of the parts of your life you can change and cause stress.

One way to do this might be to say "no" more often than not.

This is especially true when you find yourself taking on more than you can handle, as you can be frustrated by juggling multiple responsibilities.

You can reduce your stress levels by being selective about what you take on— and saying no to things that unnecessarily add to your load.

➤ **SUMMARY:** Don't try to take on more than you can. Saying no is one way your stressors can be managed.

10. That's right.

Another way to control the pressure is to stay on top of your goals and stop procrastinating:

Procrastination can lead to reactive action, allowing you to catch up scrambling. This can cause stress that negatively affects your quality of health and sleep. Get used to having a daily to-dodo list. Make realistic deadlines for yourself and work your way down the list.

Focus on the things you need to do today and give yourself blocks of uninterrupted time, as it can be difficult to toggle between tasks and multitasking.

➤ **SUMMARY:** Prioritize and make time for what needs to be done. Staying on top of your to-do list can help prevent stress-related to procrastination.

11. Take a Yoga Class:

Among all age groups, yoga has become a popular method of stress relief and exercise.

While yoga styles are different, most of them share a common goal — to join your mind and body.

Yoga does this mainly by increased awareness of body and breath.

Some studies looked at the effect of yoga on mental health. Overall, research has found that yoga can enhance mood and even be as effective in treating depression and anxiety as antidepressant drugs. However, many of these studies are limited, and questions remain as to how yoga works to reduce stress.

Generally, the value of yoga for stress and anxiety tends to be correlated with its effect on your nervous system and the reaction to stress.

It can help lower levels of cortisol, blood pressure, and heart rate, and boost gamma-amino butyric acid (GABA), a neurotransmitter that is decreased in mood disorders.

➤ **SUMMARY:** Yoga is commonly used in the reduction of pressure. It can help lower levels of stress hormone and blood pressure.

12.   Practice Attention:

Attention describes practices that anchor you to the present moment.

There are several strategies for increasing awareness, including mindfulness- based cognitive therapy, mindfulness-based reduction of stress, yoga, and meditation.

A recent study in college students indicated that carefulness could help increase self-esteem, which in effect decreases symptoms of anxiety and depression

➤ **SUMMARY:** carefulness practices may help lower anxiety and depression symptoms.

13.   Cuddle:

Cuddling, kissing, hugging, and sex can all help relieve stress. Positive physical contact may help release oxytocin and lower cortisol. This can help lower blood pressure and heart rate, both physical stress symptoms.

Ironically, humans aren't the only ones to cuddle for relief from tension. Stressed chimpanzees often cuddle friends

➤   **SUMMARY:** Positive contact from cuddling, embracing, kissing, and sex can help reduce tension by releasing oxytocin and lowering blood pressure.

14.   Listen to Soothing Music:

It can have a very relaxing effect on the body to listen to music.

By helping lower blood pressure and heart rate as well as stress hormones, slow-paced instrumental music can stimulate the response to relaxation.

Many forms of classical, Celtic, Native American, and Indian music may be particularly calming, but listening to the music you love is effective too Nature sounds can be very soothing. That's why they are often included in music for relaxation and meditation.

➤   **SUMMARY:** It can be a great way to relieve pressure by listening to music you enjoy.

15.   Deep Breathing:

Mental stress stimulates the sympathetic nervous system, meaning that your body is going into "fight-or-flight" mode.

Stress hormones are released during this reaction, and you experience physical symptoms such as a faster pulse, faster breathing, and blood vessels that are closed.

Deep breathing exercises can help stimulate the parasympathetic nervous system, which regulates the reaction to relaxation.

Many types of deep breathing exercises are available, including diaphragmatic breathing, abdominal breathing, belly breathing, and synchronized breathing.

The aim of deep breathing is to concentrate the breath perception, making it slower and deeper. If you breathe deeply through your nose, your lungs will expand fully, and your belly will rise.

This helps to slow down your heart rate, making you feel more peaceful.

➤   **SUMMARY:** Deep breathing activates the response to relaxation. You can learn to breathe deeply, using multiple methods.

16.   Have a pet:

It can help to reduce stress and improve your mood. Interacting with animals can help release oxytocin, a brain c` chemistry that encourages a positive mood. Having a pet can also help relieve anxiety by providing you with meaning, keeping you busy, and offering companionship all attributes that help to reduce fear.

➤   **SUMMARY:** A calming and enjoyable way to reduce stress is to spend time with your dog.

7.10 Easy Ways to Stay Happy and Healthy Mind

Eat Healthy

We all know that what we eat has a major impact on our physical well-being, but it also has an impact on your mental health. As the old saying goes; a healthy body makes a healthy mind, so consider your diet and what foods you can consume too much. While it is easy for those who are busy to neglect healthy food, there are plenty of fast and easy meals that are much healthier for you. Eating three meals a day will keep your energy levels up and make you feel good throughout the day. As well as eating healthy foods, drinking plenty of water will keep you hydrated and improve your metabolism.

Watch what you're drinking

While many people are drinking alcohol and caffeine to change their mood, their effect is only temporary. When the feelings of energy or excitement fade, you often feel much worse than before you drink, which has a major impact on your mental well-being. Most people only drink in moderation alcohol or caffeine that can often be good for you. Many individuals, however, continue to drink to delay the onset of these negative feelings or to avoid the underlying anxious or depressed feelings. This is very dangerous and can cause complications with long-term health and cover up existing conditions. Try to drink no more than four alcohol units a day if you're male and three if you're female and try not to drink caffeinated at night after seven o'clock.

Take any exercise

There are many different benefits to doing a little workout every day, both mental and physical. The body releases endorphins when you work out, which can greatly improve the mood. You don't have to spend a lot of money or join a gym to get some workout; walking or cycling to your destination instead of driving, cleaning the house while listening to music, and gardening are all easy ways to get blood pumping. After a while, you will find it easier to do tasks and look better, which in turn will make you feel better about yourself as a whole.

Speaking to Others

In today's world, keeping in touch with friends and family has never been easier. Feeling connected to others is an integral part of what makes us human, and neglecting this part of life can have adverse effects on your mental health. Most mental health issues find their origins in communication problems and can be supported or even avoided by maintaining strong relationships and keeping in touch with others. If you have trouble, then friends or family can provide some of the best help, so talk to them about how you feel and listen to their thoughts and emotions.

Having a Scenery Switch

Sometimes we get stuck in a rut, we all get it! Taking a vacation is a great way to relax, improve the mood, and see more of the world. Not all of us, though, are lucky enough to take off into the sun every time we feel like it. But there are a lot simpler (and less expensive) ways to take a break from our daily routine; it will help to improve your mental health as possible. Taking another route to work or simply moving around the furniture can allow the mind to experience new things and cope with different situations

Get a hobby

So much of our lives are being taken up these days by the pressures of work that we can sometimes forget what we enjoy. You may love painting, playing a musical instrument, or you've always wanted to build the country's best railway set. Taking time to dedicate yourself will help you cope with stress, focus your mind, and allow yourself to be expressed. When you feel sad, it will help you understand how you feel and make you feel much better by conveying your feelings in a drawing, song, or poem.

Acceptance of being Different

Most people are unhappy or self-conscious about their appearance, the way they speak or their background, unfair competition with others they see in magazines or on television. Such feelings can lead to a deep sense of worthlessness or even lead to conditions such as depression or eating disorder. You will be able to gain a better understanding of both your weaknesses and strengths by talking to others and expressing your feelings. If you find it helps, take five minutes a day to list the qualities that make you unique, think of one positive and then one negative, and try to accept that you are the best person you can be.

Care for Others

It's only natural to worry about the welfare of others, whoever they may be. Part of maintaining healthy relationships is getting those who matter for you back into consideration. This may be as easy as signing a' healthy' card at work or calling a friend of the elderly to see how they are. Getting a pet will constantly make you exercise these emotions as you are the person on whom they rely for food, shelter, and love. Really caring for others can help your mental health greatly and enable you to explore feelings with which you may have grown out of touch. You may even find that you enjoy it so much that you want to volunteer in the community to help others who are less fortunate than yourself, but this is just an extreme example of caring. This allows you to understand why other people care about you and why you should care about yourself.

Exercise your mind

Just like the rest of your body, to stay healthy, your brain needs exercise too. There are many different ways you can do this, from computer games to crossword puzzles. Instead of automatically measuring your bills on a calculator, first, try to calculate the amounts in your mind before checking for mechanical accuracy. Every day learning a new word is also a good way to ensure that your account remains in full working order, helping you grow older as well as in everyday life. Your brain is your most valuable tool, so it is essential to remain happy and live an active life to keep it completely functioning.

Note that support is at hand

You should feel better about yourself and yourself by taking these simple steps. However, if you feel anxious, depressed, or think you may have a mental illness, it's important to remember that there are plenty of places you can go to where you'll get plenty of support. Just like your G.P. Locally based in the community, there are many different services, such as charities and support groups. The most important thing is to let everyone know how you feel, whether it's a friend or family member, a confidential service such as the Samaritans, or professional services that your local health trust provides.

7.11 Ways to Avoid Negativity & Feel Happier

Nothing worse than filling ourselves with misery, during the day, can hurt our moods. While we can regulate our own emotions and change our attitudes, it is clear that external factors can create a negative atmosphere and dampen our states. So, to get back to a happier state, it is important to avoid triggers that create negative energy and work to quickly overcome the hurdles.

We can be happier and healthier every day by integrating healthy living factors and increasing harmful ones. Nevertheless, unexpected situations may arise where we are surrounded by negative elements, and we must maintain our composure and positive outlook to be unaffected by them. Here are 13 ways of reducing depression and starting to feel happier and relaxed when a bad mood strikes.

1)   Practice Gratitude Every Day

Gratitude will improve your mental well-being by changing your motivation and increasing your optimistic beliefs, "says Life Designer." As you change your mind to reflect on what you do and what makes you happy, your brain can begin to recognize the abundance in your life, making you feel thankful and eventually happier. Luckily, voicing and experiencing gratitude is an option that can be practiced at any time, "she says. Think about something that you are grateful for when you feel negative.

2)   Practice Radical Forgiveness

"Eliminating old resentments and forgiving not only others but also forgiving yourself is an important step to avoid negativity. Holding on to grudges can block your ability to love. After you release yourself from any past pain and love yourself, you can move on to receiving love, and then you can give love more freely,"

3)   Focus On the Present Moment Instead

Negativity comes up when they ruminate about what happened in the past and think about what might happen in the future. Everything is probably good at the moment. So, to live there, tell yourself,' what's absolutely right at this time?" I'm alive; for instance, I've got a great family, etc. You can feel a sense of peace, and then in that moment, you will have exposure to greater joy, "she says. Move past the hump of disappointment and talk of positive things that can be experienced here and now instead.

4)   Do Something That Makes You Happy

You're doing something that breaks you down and puts you in a bad mood, doing something else that doesn't seem like a burden, but a luxury will help. You will crack a negative mood and start feeling happier and more energized immediately by behaving in a positive way and doing things that you enjoy. "Switch from a task that feels like one you've got to do to one you're' wanting to do' by reconnecting with the intent of why you're doing it,"

5)   Stick to A Schedule Filled with Happy Breaks

It is a great way to rejuvenate you and promote positive attitude by taking "happiness breaks" in the day. Furthermore, you'll be better able to avoid ruminations if anxiety hits because shortly you'll have an actual event approaching to clear your mind and relieve the stress. "With consistent good behaviors and occasional periods of rejuvenation, taking care of you will help generate motivation to achieve the quality of life you want and feel happier,"

6)   Write Down Your Goals

"Evidence shows that your mind can adjust to the expectations you set, so writing down your goals increases your dedication to them and your chances of success "The mere act of setting and meeting goals will affect your satisfaction, irrespective of whether you are achieving them. The theory is that if you stick to an aim, you are more likely to enjoy the path to achieve it," she continues.

7)   Avoid Negative Self-Talk

Sometimes by not believing in ourselves or feeling too scared or unsafe to move forward, we can bring ourselves down. "To move past what holds you off, you should identify a big inhibitor the negative voice inside you that tries to keep you safe by reminding you of what may go wrong and how you may not be enough," "It's important to be aware of that voice and how it influences your way of thinking, feeling, and behaving, but don't let it run your life or let it make you worry about the past or fear the future," she advises.

8)   Have Positive Mantras to Boost Mood

Confronted with a dampened mood, having a few positive mantras to turn to is a great way to immediately elevate your spirits and channel positive energy to feel happier. Experts suggest that as long as they are powerful in their content to be useful and inspiring, these mantras can be said out loud or silently. Examples include, "You have the power to change your mood," "You're awesome and shouldn't be holding back," or "This is your day. It's time to enjoy it."

9)   Go Outside

Walking out can bring fresh oxygen into our lungs, improve our body's circulation, and clear our minds of negativity. Experts say that connecting with nature can make us immediately feel happier and more rooted in our lives, and such purpose helps eliminate negative energy and a bad mood. Go out for some fresh air next time you're angry.

10)   Buy A Plant

Research suggests that having plants at home or work can make us feel happier overall and more creative and productive in the tasks and activities we do. Holding a plant on your desk can, therefore, help to rid the mind of pessimistic, defeatist thoughts at work, and it can also suck away toxic things that can place us in a rut.

11)   Look at Something Yellow

Whether you choose to paint an office or home wall yellow to keep positive energy strong and stable every day, or you choose to buy a yellow handbag, purse, key chain or necklace, studies suggest that the yellow color can make us feel lighter and more positive. So, try to put some yellow in your life or buy a yellow flower bouquet.

12)   Avoid Negative Relationships & Be A Good Friend

You will be better able to find meaningful connections with people and build optimistic, constructive, and compassionate relationships by being a good, loyal friend who listens well and is attentive to the needs of his or her community. Evaluate toxic relationships as well and seek to separate them from such negative energy. While it might be complicated, it's going to be better for your health.

13)   Get A Little Sweaty

Experts say regular exercise can make us feel happier, more productive, more energized, and more creative overall, and this effect can last for hours after the end of your session. We can break out of negativity due to an endorphin rush and instantly improve our moods. Hit the gym to avoid an effect and start feeling happier if you feel a negative vibe approaching.

We can feel happier and more confident in a matter of minutes by doing activities and positive exercises and reciting feel-good, mood-enhancing mantras. Increasing self-esteem and confidence can make us feel stronger and more in control of our lives, emotional conditions, and the ability to have a great day.

14)   Crank the tunes:

Don't try to smile while you blast your favorite song 2. Get out: It can give you a fresh perspective just a few minutes of fresh air.

15)   Walk it out:

A brisk 20-minute walk will pump the heart and reduce stress.

16)   Use your accessories to make a statement:

A bold statement necklace, your shades of too-cool-for-school, or your favorite kicks can be all you need to turn around a' blah' day.

17)   Make a boost for yourself:

Healthy nutrients! Fruit, veggies, and protein we're talking about. Your brain will follow when your body feels good.

18)   Leave a note:

Make somebody's day on the mirror of the bathroom by leaving a "you're beautiful" note.

19) Do something:

Whether you're sending an email or clearing the clutter off your table in the dining room, just getting one tiny little thing off your to-do list and on the' it's done' menu will give you a huge mental sigh of relief.

20) Say, "thank you."

Even this little act of gratitude will increase your positive attitude.

21) Learn something new:

Whether reading a wiki about a topic you're interested in or watching a quick YouTube tutorial, there's plenty of ways to learn things quickly and on the go. Yes, even the courses of happiness! :) Let it go: by detaching yourself from past negativity, you can boost your satisfaction.

22) Straighten yourself up!

Our stance dictates how we feel, so make it straight and walk like a boss!

23) Try something new:

Break your routine and mix up stuff! It can be as simple as walking down another street— anything to get off the autopilot and be there where you are.

24)   Spend money:

According to Harvard professor Mike Norton, the trick is you have to spend it on someone else to get the' feel excellent' benefits.

25)   Text a friend:

Getting to a friend and letting them know how awesome they are will also make you feel awesome.

26)   Make plans:

Having something to look forward to, even making plans with a friend to grab a cup of coffee, makes you happier. Anticipation is like happiness's secret weapon.

27)   Help somebody:

Do you feel down? One of the fastest ways to get back is to do something beautiful for someone else. Bonus, when it's random and not expected of you, feel-good points.

28)   Stop comparing yourself:

You're always going to pick those at the top to compare with. No wonder you feel like you're short! It's much more productive to focus on the things you've accomplished.

29)   Smile:

In one study, subjects who smiled after a stressful activity control their heart rate faster than those who didn't. Even if you smile fake, it works!

30)   Power color:

Of course, whilst we are partial to orange, whatever your favorite color may be, embrace it. Bonus: Give yourself a flower in your favorite color when you feel down. The room and your outlook will be brightened.

31)   Treat yourself:

Sometimes, all we need to break out of a rut is a tiny little luxury in our day.

32)   Read something:

Whether it's your favorite guilty-pleasure celebrity gossip mag or taking a couple of moments to indulge in something you really enjoy will give you a decisive energy burst. You could learn something more

33)   Cute overload:

Seeing something sweet makes we smile, making us happier in turn. The twitter feed for the Cute Emergency will save a bad day as fast as you can say "Golden Retriever puppy."

8. Conclusion

There are different approaches around the world to mental health and mental illness. Most health professionals agree on a similar set of mental health issues clinical diagnoses and treatments. Within our data, we have chosen to reflect this approach, as these are the terminology and treatment models.

Not everyone, though, finds it helpful to think this way about their mental health. You may have different ideas about how best to cope, depending on your traditions and beliefs. Emotional well-being is closely linked to religious or spiritual life in many cultures. And your challenging encounters may be just one aspect of your overall understanding of your identity.

As many people have told us that this is beneficial for them. But you may be more familiar with words like "poor emotional wellbeing," "overloaded," "burnt out," or "overwhelmed." Or you may find that words like' mental disease' or' mental health issues ' better describe your experiences or are more comfortable to explain to others in your life.

Note that you are not alone when you feel overwhelmed by tension. You'll be back to living a safe, happy life in no time with a few lifestyle changes and support from a counselor you trust. You're stronger than any stressor on your way. Take today's first step. Try to make your life better

Nonetheless, you know your perspectives, and whatever words you choose to use, we hope that when considering different care and support choices, you can find the information helpful in this book.

CPSIA information can be obtained
at www.ICGtesting.com
Printed in the USA
BVHW040002190221
600507BV00012B/954